RAMBLING THROUGH THE EMERALD ISLE

Mary E. Heaton

A Russian Hill Press Book
United States • United Kingdom • Australia

Russian Hill Press

The publisher is not responsible for websites (or their content) that are not owned by the publisher.

Designer: Christine McCall
Author's Photo: Lisa Foote
Ireland Photos: Terry Tunnington

LCCN: 2014952184

ISBN: 978-0-9911973-8-5

To my beloved husband, Duane.

Rambling Through the Emerald Isle

INTRODUCTION

Dear Reader,

You may have chosen to read this memoir because you are interested in Ireland. Maybe you are of Irish ancestry, or perhaps you want to learn about this beautiful country.

Whatever the case, my intention is to take you, along with my daughter Alana, on our twelve-day journey, rambling through the Emerald Isle.

My mother, Kathleen Claffy (Claffey, as it was spelled by my ancestors), and her sister, Jane, are the two people who instilled in me the desire to go to Ireland. When I was young, my mom spoke fondly of her mother's parents who were from Ireland, as well as her great-grandparents on her father's side. I have always felt a connection to all things Irish because Mom and Aunt Jane brought it into our home. We had many fun St. Patrick's Day celebrations growing up, eating green pancakes, drinking green milk, or green beer, depending on our age.

My mom told me many times over the years that she wanted to go to Ireland, but she never went and that made her sad. Raising seven children—Colleen, Peggy, Patrick, Kathleen, Christopher, Mark, and me—Mom and Dad never had the extra money for trips to Europe.

When I left for Ireland at the end of 2006, my mother was seventy-nine years old. By that time, she had gone blind from macular degeneration and was very frail from osteoporosis, so she wasn't able to come with me. I told her that when I got back, I would describe to her in detail all the places I visited so that she could see them in her mind's eye.

Because of my mother's blindness, I consciously and meticulously etched into my memory all the details of our trip. Knowing Mom couldn't look at pictures or flip through brochures to complete her mental picture of a place, it fell to me to provide all the precise particulars. I believe this, coupled with the actual recounting of our Irish adventures in the following weeks and months, enabled me to write the story years later without the help of a journal. Chapter One, "The Gift," was written several years before the rest of this memoir. It had to be included here because it is the reason my daughter and I went to Ireland.

The remainder of this narrative came to me later as a result of a writing prompt from my creative writing teacher, Susan Wilson, who challenged her students to write about a vacation experience. I hope you will find my story funny, heartwarming, and informative.

May the luck of the Irish be with you.

Mary Heaton (née Hansen)
Descendent from the clans of Claffey, O'Neill, Donohue, Quinn, Carroll, and Mahoney

CHAPTER 1
The Gift

IN OCTOBER OF 2004, MY husband, Duane, went for his annual checkup with his primary care physician, Dr. Nguyen, at the Kaiser Clinic in our hometown of Livermore, California. His doctor called several days later and told him to come in and repeat the bloodwork. The following week, Dr. Nguyen called again and wanted the tests repeated. By the third phone call, we knew something wasn't right. Dr. Nguyen sent a referral for Duane to see a hematologist. Duane was scheduled for an appointment on November 24 at Kaiser Hospital in Walnut Creek, California.

We waited anxiously for the appointment day to arrive and drove the twenty-five miles to the hospital. As we walked up to the Hematology Department, we noticed it was called the

Hematology/Oncology Department, and we became even more nervous.

We met Dr. Simmons, a hematologist/oncologist, and he seemed nice. He spoke with us about Duane's bloodwork and said, "Mr. Heaton, your blood counts are severely low. You may have a blood disease, but I need to examine you first."

After the examination, Dr. Simmons looked Duane right in the eye and said, "Mr. Heaton, you have lymphoma. I will order more tests to determine what type of lymphoma you have because there are thirty-nine different types."

Duane asked him, "How can you tell I have lymphoma?"

"Well, I can feel that you have enlarged lymph nodes in your neck, under your arms, and in your groin area. That, coupled with your bloodwork, tells me that is what you have," he said with a concerned look.

We left the appointment in shock. Duane was forty-seven years old and had none of the obvious symptoms of cancer, such as fatigue, night sweats, and loss of appetite. After many tests, we learned that Duane had indolent follicular lymphoma. He was a stage four plus, and if you know anything about cancer, you know there is no stage five.

The cancer was in the lymph nodes in his neck, lungs, abdomen, spleen, and groin, as well as in his bone marrow. He needed chemotherapy as soon as possible.

So, in January of 2005, Duane began a six-month regimen of chemotherapy at Walnut Creek Kaiser, a cycle every three weeks. I took the day off from work and went with him, bringing reading material, snacks, and playing cards. Most of the time, Duane slept, and I sat and read or crocheted. It was a long, grueling process.

Sometimes, we were in the chemotherapy infusion unit in Walnut Creek for six hours at a time. The chemo made Duane tired and irritable. He lost his hair, twenty pounds, and his pink coloring.

After six months, the doctor ordered a CT scan. The resulting scan showed no evidence of the disease. The cancer was gone, and we were thrilled. Duane was instructed to return for checkups every three months, or sooner should the cancer return, for the next five years.

A year later, Dr. Simmons noticed that Duane's blood counts were off again. He ordered another CT scan, and the results showed that Duane's spleen was enlarged.

The doctor recommended that Duane have more chemo, but we wanted a second opinion. His oncologist was able to get permission from Kaiser to send my husband to Stanford in Palo Alto,

California, one of the most well respected teaching hospitals in the United States.

We drove thirty-six miles to Stanford Hospital in October of 2006. We met with a doctor who specialized in lymphoma; her name was Dr. Ganjoo. She had read all of Duane's records and looked at his scans. She said, "Mr. Heaton, you need to have a splenectomy. Your spleen is trapping all of your platelets. They are the cells that clot the blood. Your spleen needs to be removed as soon as possible. If you have any more chemotherapy right now, it will kill you because your immune system is completely depleted."

We went back to Dr. Simmons at Kaiser after he received the records from Stanford, and he ordered the surgery for January of 2007. He thought it best to have the splenectomy after the holidays so Duane could be with his family during Christmas. Duane was tiring easily because his blood counts were getting dangerously low. If he got a bad cut or some kind of serious internal injury, he would not have enough platelets to clot his blood and could possibly hemorrhage to death.

During that year, I had been through many ups and downs and was doing my best to be a supportive caregiver and a good mother to my five children. Our oldest daughter, Jill, was living away from home at the time. I was also working half days as a primary school teacher at Valley Montessori School in Livermore. It was a very emotional and tough time for Duane and me.

As I came home from work one day in early November, Duane called me into the backyard, so the boys couldn't hear what he had to say to me. He had our family calendar in his hand. I asked him, "What's up?"

"I want to talk with you about something," he said with a concerned look.

"Sure. Why do you have the calendar in your hand?"

"Mary, I have booked a flight for you to go visit our daughter Alana in Prague on December 16," he said, pointing at the day on the calendar. "You will stay there four days and then you and she are going to fly to Ireland and stay there for twelve days and then fly home on the first of January."

I stared at him and said, "What are you talking about? I can't leave you. You're not doing well, and I can't leave our sons at Christmas." At the time, our boys were 8, 13, and 15 years old.

Duane said, "Yes, you must go. I already called Alana and set it up with her."

Alana was studying abroad in Prague at the time. I looked at Duane with tears in my eyes and said, "I can't go, what if you…?" I couldn't finish my sentence, but he knew what I was going to say.

He looked at me beseechingly. "Mary, that's why you have to go. If I die during the surgery, you won't be able to go to Ireland for a long time, or maybe you'll never make it there. You will be taking care of the kids and may not be able to afford to travel. I know it has always been your dream to go to Ireland. You have to go. It's my gift to you."

As I stood crying in my husband's arms, I knew that I must accept his gift because it was given to me out of pure, selfless love. I needed to honor his gift because I needed to honor him.

CHAPTER 2
Planning the Trip

ONCE I FINALLY COMMITTED TO going on the trip, and the idea sunk into my brain, I realized Alana and I needed to start planning. This proved to be difficult because she was living in Prague in the Czech Republic, and I was home in Livermore. It was the second week in November 2006, and I was leaving for Europe on December 16, only a month away. I needed to start doing some research on what to see and where to stay in Ireland because I was running out of time. I was teaching at Valley Montessori School in town and took care of my three sons and husband, so I was quite a busy woman. I had to plan the trip at night and on the weekends.

I wanted Alana's input, but it was expensive to call her on the phone, so we set up a few Skype dates where she went to a coffee shop with Wi-Fi. We didn't have video, which was too bad, but we talked for free and that was a plus. We emailed each other and set up a Skype date for Sunday, November 26, 10:00 a.m., California time, 7:00 p.m., Prague time.

"Hi, Alana. I can't believe that I get to come and visit you. It is less than a month away. It has been four long months since you left the U.S."

"I know, Mom. Isn't it great? I was so excited when Dad called and told me about his plan. I couldn't wait until he finally told you, so I could talk to you about it."

"I really didn't want to go at first, because, you know, he is very sick."

"I know Mom, I thought about that too, but he insisted."

"Yes, he is making me go because it is his gift to me."

"I know Mom. He is a great guy to do that for you and me."

"He sure is. Well, we better start talking about where I am going to stay in Prague."

"I have already found a few hotels in my area, so I will send you the links via email and you can choose one because, unfortunately, you can't stay in my apartment. The school won't allow it. Plus, I have a roommate."

"That's fine, Alana. As far as Ireland goes, I want to go to all the places where I know our ancestors came from—Cork, Galway, and Athlone. I looked at the map of Ireland, and to be most efficient, we should fly into Cork and then drive in a clockwise fashion up the West Coast to Galway and then straight through the middle of the country to Athlone and then on to Dublin. We can fly back home from the Dublin airport. It makes the most sense."

"That sounds great, Mom. Let's start looking up places to stay in all those cities."

Now that we had an outline, Alana and I did our own research about where to visit and stay in Ireland. We shared our findings with each other by computer, sending links about interesting places to visit along the way to each of our destinations. This proved to be a very efficient way to plan our trip.

It was fun to come home from work to find emails from Alana about beautiful places to go in Ireland. Because I was going to be doing the driving, I insisted that we stay two nights in each town. This way, the bulk of the driving would be limited to every other day. Because Ireland is a small country, I wasn't going to have to drive more than two hours at a time. It takes roughly three and one-half hours to drive from the West Coast of Ireland to the East Coast. It is so different from the

USA, where it takes forty-four hours to drive from San Francisco on the West Coast to New York City on the East Coast.

You see, I am not fond of driving, but I figured that we were going to be traveling mostly in the countryside, and I thought, how difficult can it be? Alana had gotten her license when she was seventeen but hadn't driven much because she had been in college the last three years and didn't own a car. To see the sights in the country, we had to rent a car. So that's what we were going to do.

Alana and I pooled our information and made our reservations at the various B&Bs online. Finally, we were all set to go to Ireland.

CHAPTER 3
Flying to Europe

A WEEK BEFORE CHRISTMAS, I was standing in line waiting to board a Lufthansa plane at San Francisco International Airport. I was crying my eyes out because I was flying to the Czech Republic by myself. To tell you the honest truth, I was scared to death, going without my husband and sons. But Duane gave me a selfless gift that I had to honor.

I was flying to Prague first to attend Alana's graduation from the Communications Abroad Program at Charles University. Together, we were flying to Ireland to spend twelve days touring our ancestral home. Going to Ireland had always been on my bucket list, but I was not traveling under the best circumstances. My husband was going to have surgery in a month's time, and I didn't know if he was going to survive it. I may not have another chance to go to Europe, ever. I had to go, right? I was desperately trying to convince myself that we all were going to be fine through this situation, but I had my doubts.

I was trying to hide my sobs as I looked back one last time at Duane and the boys waving good-bye to me. Taking a few deep breaths, I boarded the plane and hesitantly sat in my assigned seat. I continued to take deep breaths to calm myself down when I noticed a young couple with two small children, an infant and a toddler, sitting across from me. Boy, this is going to be long flight, I thought to myself, and I was right. The first three hours of the flight, the toddler screamed and then, gratefully, she fell asleep. But then her brother woke up, and he cried for the next three hours until it was his sister's turn again.

You get the picture. Okay, so I didn't sleep a wink on the eleven-hour flight to Frankfurt, which was my first stop on the way to Prague. I felt sorry for the young couple; at least I didn't have to take care of children on a transatlantic flight.

Once I arrived in Germany, I had a two-hour layover in Frankfurt. The antiquated airport was claustrophobic with very narrow passageways. It was strange to hear most people speaking German or other languages. Many were smoking cigarettes, which I am allergic to. I felt alone and frightened as

I tried to find the correct terminal. I finally found the right gate and sat there by myself. I pulled out my husband's iPod. I had never used one, but he had given me a quick lesson before I left home on how to turn it on and off. He was so kind to download all the episodes of *Grey's Anatomy* so that I could pass the time during my layover. Once I started watching the show, I quickly felt more relaxed.

When the time came to depart, I took a little hopper plane from Frankfurt to Prague. Thankfully, it was a very quick flight, only forty-five minutes. I disembarked the plane outside—no insulated walkways here—and trotted inside the terminal to warm myself. The airport was quite beautiful, open and airy and very modern looking, not at all what I expected. It was the complete opposite from the Frankfurt airport, which was so unattractive and scary.

I frantically did a 360 looking for my daughter, Alana. She wasn't there. "Oh, crap. What should I do?" I said out loud, knowing there wasn't another soul within earshot who could understand me. I didn't know a word of Czech, so I just sat at the gate for forty-five minutes.

Then I thought, maybe she is in another part of the terminal waiting for me. I started walking when I saw the confused traveler's lifeline, a staffed white courtesy phone.

I walked up to the young woman at the counter and asked, "Do you speak English?"

"Yiz, I do, Ma'am."

"Thank goodness."

"I know vittle bit."

"I am looking for my daughter, Alana Miller. Will you please call for her on the loudspeaker?"

"Yiz." She picked up the phone and announced, "Vill, Ilona Millar coom to the vhite curtezy phon dezk, pleeze."

Hallelujah. It worked. I saw Alana walking around the corner towards me, looking so cute with her short, black hair cut in a chic style, and her chocolate-brown eyes alive with excitement. She was wearing a thick gray coat and gold scarf that she had knitted herself. Alana is a few inches shorter than I and stands at five-feet two inches. The most beautiful fair skin and stunning dark eyebrows enhance her lovely oval face. With similar facial features and curvy figures, we definitely look like mother and daughter; however, I have short blonde hair, aqua blue eyes, and a rosy complexion.

I threw myself into her arms. "It's so great to see you, Honey. I'm really out of my comfort zone, you know?"

"Oh, Mom, you're okay," she said laughing. "You made it. Now let's get on the Metro and go to my apartment. I am so sorry I was late getting here. It took a lot longer than I expected."

"That's okay, Alana. At least you are here now," I said gratefully.

During the next three days, we had a wonderful time strolling around the medieval cobblestone streets of Prague. We visited the Prague Castle, built in AD 970. It was a commanding citadel on top of the highest point in the city with a breathtaking view of terra cotta tiled rooftops. We walked over the St. Charles Bridge, which spans the beautiful Vltava River. We explored cemeteries and museums and ate delicious vegetarian food. (My daughter was a vegetarian at the time.) The weather was extremely mild for that time of year, sunny and in the fifties with no precipitation.

I noticed many older women with hair dyed an atrocious color of red and asked my daughter about it. She laughed and said, "It's called 'Commie Red' because that was the only hair dye available during the time of Communism here. It seems to be the only hair dye that the older women still use."

"I guess old habits die hard," I said, laughing. "No pun intended."

I attended Alana's heartwarming graduation ceremony from the four-month program, and I met some of her classmates. Her roommate, Pavla, was almost six feet tall and gorgeous, with long, wavy blonde hair. She was a young Czech woman who spoke fluent Spanish. Pavla, too, was a vegetarian who loved to Salsa dance. Alana's classmate, Steph, was from Wisconsin. A petite girl with short, dark hair and a lovely smile, she and Alana had become good friends during their stay in Prague. Steph was also going to Ireland before she went back to the States.

Pavla had a little going-away party for Alana the day we left for Ireland. Steph was going to share a taxi to the airport though we weren't on the same flight.

"Alana, we need to get going. Please call a taxi. It's getting late," I said impatiently.

The taxi finally arrived at six o'clock and our flight was leaving at seven-thirty. I felt stressed.

"Mom, don't worry. We have plenty of time," she said calmly.

On the way to the airport, we hit a traffic jam. It was bumper to bumper, and I kept looking at my watch. We finally arrived at the scene of an accident, and the taxi driver asked the police officer what happened.

He replied, "A vittle girl vaz hit by car and kilt." Alana, Steph, and I sat in total silence the rest of the way to the airport.

We quickly paid and thanked the cab driver and ran as fast as we could to the Aer Lingus counter. It was a few minutes after seven when we finally reached the ticket agent. I was breathing hard as I said, "We are on Flight 870 to Cork, Ireland."

"I om verry sorry, but yu ar' too late. The fleit haz boarted and is clozed," the agent said apologetically.

Alana and I looked at each other. "What are we going to do now?"

Just then the ticket agent said excitedly, "Vait a minute, the fleit haz been delayet due to denze fog at Cork airport."

"Woo-hoo," we shouted in unison. We had to wait two hours before we took off, but that was fine with me. We met an Irish priest while sitting in the waiting area who was kind and talked to us about great places to visit in his home country. He was about five feet six inches with a full head of snow-white hair. His stiff priest collar fit tightly around his thick neck. His blue eyes twinkled and his ruddy face looked friendly.

"Where are yu tu goin' in Ireland?"

"Well, we're starting out in Cork, heading to Tralee, Connemara, straight across to Athlone, and on to Dublin. I chose all these places because those are the cities that our ancestors came from, except Dublin," I said with excitement.

"Ah, yes. Well, when yur in Cork yu must go tu the little town of Cobh. It sounds like 'Cove' but spelled in Irish, it is C-o-b-h. It is such a wonderful town. Yu have tu take the train, but 'tis easy enough. 'Tis by the sea and so beautiful."

"That sounds nice. We should do that, Alana."

"Did yu know that Alana means beautiful child in Gaelic?" said the priest.

"Actually, I do know. That is why I named her that. Her middle name is Maria, after me."

"Well, wut a lovely name tha' 'tis."

"Thank you, Father."

"I teach at University College in Cork. I am a professor of history there."

"Oh, that's nice. That is why you know so much," I said, smiling.

Finally, over the loudspeaker, we heard that our plane was boarding.

"Well, Ladies, nice to meet you and have a wonderful time in Ireland."

"Thank you, Father, I am sure we will. Take care."

CHAPTER 4
Cork

WE DIDN'T GET TO IRELAND until 1:00 a.m., and the rental car agency closed at 11:00 p.m. Because we were spending the next two nights in Cork, we needed to find a taxi to take us to the hostel Alana had picked out for our first night. We found a cab right away and told the cabbie where we wanted to go.

He was a very chatty man with a thick Irish brogue. He asked us, "What the 'ell ar' yu tu doin' 'lone at thus time of night?"

I explained that we had come from Prague and why we were delayed. I said, "We were supposed to get a rental car, but the place was closed."

"Will that's gut, most American tourists get intu accidents and die cause yu don' know how to drive on the right side of the road."

"Oh, great," I said. "That is just what I needed to hear."

"So, wher's yur husband?"

"Oh, he is home with my three sons. He gave this trip to me as a Christmas present. You see my daughter here was studying in Prague and I went to her graduation and my husband thought it would be nice for me to go and then spend time in Ireland with her."

"So, yur husband and sons are bachin' it at home, are they? Thur gettin' a bit of time off from the bitches," he said, then laughed. Alana and I laughed along with him.

We pulled up to our hostel, and I was not impressed. It looked like a dive, but I imagine at 1:30 a.m. in a foreign country, everything looks a bit creepy. We paid the cabby, thanked him for the ride, and carried our bags into the hostel.

We were both exhausted from the long day. I didn't get much sleep that night. After a few hours, I had to go to the bathroom, and my scary thoughts were getting the best of me. I remembered a *Law and Order* episode where two young women were staying in a seedy hotel in New York, and one had to go to the bathroom. She couldn't lock the hotel door behind her and when she returned to the room, her friend had been murdered.

Well, like the show, I couldn't lock the door

behind me. I didn't want to leave my daughter in an unlocked room, but I had to go to the bathroom. I lay awake for a while and then I thought, I would go as quickly as possible and race back. And that's what I did.

I was back in a flash. Alana was just fine but my sleep deprivation was really getting to me.

The next morning I felt much better. The sun was shining, and it was quite comfortable outside wearing just a light sweater—a rare day in Ireland on December 20.

Cork is the third largest city in Ireland with over 119,000 people. The buildings are painted in bright colors of green, blue, and red. Many shops and pubs line the streets of Cork. The hostel we stayed at was on the edge of town, and we were able to walk all over the city easily. We found a cute little restaurant and ate a huge scrumptious breakfast. I was starving.

After breakfast, we began strolling up and down the streets of Cork; we came upon a lovely old church called St. Fin Barre's Cathedral. As we entered the sanctuary, I said to Alana, "I wonder if my great-great-grandmother Johannah Mahoney ever sat on one of these wooden pews. She was born in 1843, in Cork, and the church was completed in 1879. It's possible that she attended Mass here."

We read that William Burges, a designer, won the job in an architectural competition in 1863. The church took seven years to build and was designed in the Gothic-Revival style. We gazed up at the lovely, colorful stained glass windows and walked up to the altar, automatically making the sign of the cross and kneeling, as we were taught to do in Catechism class when we were young. It's funny how traditions trigger our reflexes.

We left the cathedral and walked on a stone bridge over the River Lee to find the English Market. We heard that it was a great place to have lunch. We entered the two-story building on the lower level. Stalls of vegetables, fruit, meat, and cheeses were everywhere, a wonderful variety of food. We found a restaurant upstairs with a small table available. Alana ordered a vegetarian dish. I ordered the Irish lamb stew, one of my favorite dishes. I cooked lamb every so often at home when Alana was young, and she enjoyed it. So, my vegetarian daughter broke down and tasted my stew and loved it.

Alana and I spent the day rambling around the streets of Cork, and later that afternoon, walked to the Cork train station searching for a train to Cobh. We took the 3:30 p.m. train and rode out of the city, savoring the bucolic countryside. Upon our arrival, Alana and I realized we should have come earlier in the day because the sun was getting low in the sky. I remembered the nice priest at the Prague airport telling us there was a museum in Cobh honoring the victims of the Titanic voyage. The museum was a short walk from the train station. You can imagine our disappointment finding it closed.

Fortunately for us, photos and historical information written on wall plaques could be seen through the museum's windows. Cobh was the very last port the Titanic left from before heading out to sea. A memorial is located outside the museum to honor the victims.

Walking along the water's edge, Alana and I noticed an absence of people in town. We had the strange feeling of strolling into an episode from the *Twilight Zone*. The pride and joy of Cobh was a magnificent church perched high upon a hilltop in the center of town, which towered over all the other structures. Alana and I were intrigued and had to see the gorgeous church. We found a very long stone staircase that led to the top of the hill. When we reached the huge wooden doors of the church, it was twilight. Spotlights shone upon the magnificent building.

A sign outside read: Saint Colman Cathedral. After climbing all those stairs, we hoped to find it unlocked. I pulled on the huge brass handle, and the door opened to a gigantic sanctuary. Not a soul was inside. It was so quiet as Alana and I walked around the interior, appreciating the architecture and the beautiful statues of the saints. The construction of the church began in 1868, but it wasn't completed until 1915, a total of 47 years. Built in the Gothic-Revival style, it was something to behold.

When we left the cathedral it was evening. We needed to get back to the station to catch the six o'clock train back to Cork. We had to walk down all those stone stairs in the dark, and while I was a little nervous, we did just fine. We got to the train station in time and made it back to Cork safe and sound, but we were exhausted from the long day.

The next day we called a cab to take us to the airport, so we could pick up our rental car. We had rented a Nissan Micra, which looks just like its name sounds—very small. The driver's seat was on the right side and the stick shift on the left. I am left-handed, so the stick on the left didn't bother me, but driving on the other side of the road was going to be a challenge. What was I thinking, volunteering to drive in Ireland?

I started out driving in the parking lot and I was okay, but there was a roundabout as we drove away from the airport. Instead of going clockwise, as I was supposed to in Ireland, I started going counter clockwise as I would do in the States. Cars were honking, and tires were screeching, and I was freaking out.

"Mom, you need to calm down," Alana pleaded.

"I am trying to, Honey," I cried out. But it was awful. I took a few deep breaths and corrected my mistake, much to the relief of the angry motorists around me.

Once I got on the highway I began to breathe more easily.

"Mom, there's the turn off for the Blarney Stone," Alana said with excitement.

"We're not getting off this road. I need to go straight for a while," I snapped, and Alana kept quiet after that.

We drove about an hour and stopped in Killarney to have lunch. My hands and fingers were sore from gripping the steering wheel so tightly, and I needed food. We had a few toasties at a small café. Toasties are very popular in Ireland; they are basically a grilled cheese sandwich with ham inside. They were delicious.

After lunch Alana and I went into a beautiful shop called the Aran Sweater Market which sold skein wool as well as sweaters. I have a weakness for both. I had always wanted an Irish woolen sweater, but they were too expensive, so I never bought one. It was the one and only item that I wanted to purchase for myself while visiting Ireland.

This shop had hundreds of sweaters in all the colors of the rainbow. How was I going to choose? The store had the traditional Irish fisherman's sweaters, cream-colored, dye-free pullovers, in many different patterns. In fact, I found that each clan has its own stitch pattern. The sweaters were stacked in neat rows along the wall, separated by clan surnames like O'Brien, Casey, O'Malley, Joyce, and Boyle above them. In Ireland these sweaters are called jumpers or guernseys.

I looked through all the Irish surnames, and unfortunately, they didn't have a Claffey-patterned sweater. I decided that I didn't want a pullover sweater after all. I wanted one with buttons, so that eliminated three-quarters of the garments in the shop. I continued to search for the perfect one and then I spotted it: a periwinkle cardigan with mother-of-pearl buttons, beautifully made with soft Merino wool.

With my purchase in hand, we headed off to Tralee, our destination for that day.

Driving through the gorgeous countryside, we took in the green hills, craggy mountains, and lovely pine trees in groves that appeared along the roadway unexpectedly. Cars kept trying to pass me and I let them. The speed limit was 100 kph, which is about 62 mph, but in Ireland the country roads are incredibly narrow with hedgerows along the roadways. There are no shoulders to pull off on. It was very scary to drive around.

Well, at one point I started getting panicky again and Alana said, "Mom, are you okay?"

I murmured, "No, I'm not."

Then all of a sudden Alana began singing, "Raindrops on roses…" I quickly looked over at her and smiled, then laughed and began to sing with her.

After we finished the song I said, "Thank you, Honey. That song really calmed me down."

"Well, when I was little and scared you always sang that song to me to make me feel better. It always worked."

I felt so much love for my daughter that day. She was a great traveling companion and a best friend. What a true gift my husband had given me.

We made it to Tralee, where our B&B was located, around 4:00 p.m. It was a lovely Victorian house painted dove gray with cream trim. We knocked on the door, but no one answered. Alana and I were standing on the porch when a young man came walking around from the back of the inn and said, "Cun I hulp yu?"

"Yes, we booked a room here for two nights and we drove from Cork today."

"My ma's not here right now. She runs the place, but I'll let yu in."

Thank God. I needed to rest. I hadn't had much sleep in the last four days. We brought our luggage in and noticed there was a pub adjacent to the B&B. The sign read, "Open at 5 PM."

Alana and I settled in. At five o'clock I said, "Let's go to the pub and get something to eat. I'm starving." We entered the quaint whitewashed building and went up to the woman at the bar.

I introduced Alana and myself. She said, "Oh, yur the lady and her girl who's sta'n' here. My name is Colleen and I run thu place."

I said with as much control as I could muster at the time, "Nice to meet you. You have a beautiful B&B. May I have a shot of Jameson whiskey, please."

"Are yu sure now, no water or ice?"

"No. Straight please. It's been a difficult day. I had to drive on the other side of the road all day, and I am stressed out."

"Oh, me son lives in South Carolina and I niver drive meself over there. Yu deserve a whiskey."

She handed me my drink. I downed it and, slammed the shot glass on the wooden bar, and said, "Ahhh."

CHAPTER 5
Tralee

AFTER DRINKING MY SHOT OF Jameson's Irish whiskey, I could feel the alcohol relaxing my muscles and I felt calmer. I instantly realized that I was starving. I asked Colleen, "May we see a menu please?"

"Oh, wa don' serve food here in the pub, sorry dear."

"Colleen, I will pay whatever you want. I can't go out and drive in the dark. I can barely drive in daylight."

Seeing my desperation, she said, "I'll see wha' I cun do." Colleen left the bar and came back in a few minutes. "I 'av sum shepherd's pie and sum chips, will tha' suit ya?"

"That sounds wonderful. Thank you so much," I said with gratitude.

She went back into the kitchen. After a few minutes, she returned and said, "My daughter will bring out the food tu yu in about ten minutes." I proceeded to order another shot of whiskey for good measure, and Alana ordered a pint of beer. We found a table and sat, trying to wait patiently for our food. We noticed a few older Irishmen sitting at the bar. They all looked to be in their seventies. We were the only women in the place, and it felt peculiar. Colleen's daughter came out with a tray of food. She was about Alana's age, 19. "Here's yur food. Where are yu Ladies from?" she asked.

"We're from California," Alana said.

"Oh, tha's nice. I have always wanted tu go thur. Maybe one day I will."

"I am sure you will. What's your name?" Alana asked.

"My name is Siobhan."

"Well, thank you so much for the food. We are so hungry, and it tastes delicious," I said.

"Oh, yur welcome. I hope yu 'av a nice time in Ireland."

"Thank you, Siobhan. I'm sure we will," I said.

The food was outstanding. The shepherd's pie had a flaky crust with tender beef inside. The chips were fried golden brown and not too crisp, just the way I like them. She also put a generous serving of peas on each of our plates. Mind you, I hate peas, but I ate every last one of them. I guess Irish peas taste better than American ones.

"Why does food always taste so extra good when you are starving, Alana?"

"I don't know Mom, but I am sure glad they had some to serve to us. Otherwise, we would have been out of luck."

"You've got that right. I would have had to drink my dinner instead," I said laughing.

After we finished our food, we decided to head off to bed. It had been a very long and stressful day, and I was certainly ready to lay my body down to rest. As we were walking out the door, Colleen asked, "Would yu be likin' a traditional Irish breakfast in the mornin'?"

I replied, "Sure, that sounds great." Not bothering to ask exactly what it was, I was just happy I didn't have to drive anywhere to get it.

I woke up feeling like a new person because I had finally gotten a good night's sleep. I think the whiskey helped me out with that. Alana and I showered, dressed, and walked into the dining room for breakfast. Colleen greeted us warmly and asked, "Would you like sum tea?"

"Yes," I said. "That would be wonderful."

She brought us an assortment of teas and said, "Your breakfast will be out in a few minutes, Ladies."

While Alana and I sipped our tea, we took in our surroundings. The dining room was furnished with formal Victorian-era furniture. On the walls was wallpaper colored moss green and antique gold. A lovely crystal chandelier hung above us. We sat at a large, oval antique table with carved legs. The matching chairs had cushions upholstered in burgundy velvet.

Colleen carried in a sterling silver tray with our traditional Irish breakfast: fried eggs, sausage, black pudding, white pudding, brown bread, white toast, fried tomatoes and rashers. It's a good thing I didn't know what black and white pudding was until later, because I would not have eaten it. Black pudding is made of pork meat, fat, bread, oatmeal, and pig's blood. White pudding contains all of the same ingredients, except for the blood. Rashers, I found out, are bacon slices. Well, Alana and I tried our best, but we barely made a dent. When we told Colleen we were finished, she looked disappointedly at our plates.

"Colleen, I am so sorry we didn't eat more."

"Will t'morrow I will make somethin' smaller, like porridge." She turned heel and walked back to the kitchen quickly. We felt terrible to waste the food, but we had no idea there would be so much.

Alana and I spread the map of Ireland on the dining room table and began planning our route for the day. We chose to visit the town of Dingle and the Ring of Kerry, neither of which was too far away. Our B&B was located on the outskirts of Tralee. Dingle was about 25 miles away. I wanted to get an early start so we went back to our room, grabbed our purses, and eagerly headed out. With newfound courage, I was ready for the drive. Luckily, it was Christmas week so not too many people were out and about on the country roads. It was a clear, sunny day.

On our way out of Tralee, we saw a gigantic windmill called the Blennerville Windmill. It looked just like the ones I had seen in pictures of Holland. It is the largest functioning mill in Ireland and Britain at seventy feet tall. An English settler named Sir Rowland Blennerhassett built it in 1800. Rowland's wife, Milicent, was killed when the canvas-covered blades of the windmill struck her. Blennerhassett's windmill was primarily used to grind corn, much of which was sent to England. In the early 1800s there were over 100 working windmills, but by 1850, with the introduction of steam engines, windmills went out of fashion. In 1849 the Blennerville Windmill was abandoned and fell derelict until 1982, when the Urban Council of Tralee decided to restore it for the tourism industry. Blennerville was the main port of emigration during the Great Potato Famine of 1845-1848.

"It is quite possible that some of our ancestors, maybe the O'Neills from Galway, left Ireland to come to America from this very port," I said to Alana.

Because of all the driving I did the day before, I had a much easier time and was much more confident. We followed the signs for Dingle and headed up the Slieve Mish Mountains, which would be considered hills by California standards. The road was winding. We rarely saw other cars, but if we did, I let them pass. Alana and I got a true appreciation of the Irish countryside. When we arrived at the top of the mountain, we could see Dingle Bay below. At the sight of it, I was overcome with emotion and began to cry.

"Mom, what's wrong? Why are you crying?"

I pulled over to the side of the road and said, "They are tears of joy, Alana. I am so happy to be here with you. Duane gave me such a wonderful gift. I am also thinking of my mother and how much she wanted to visit Ireland, but she never made it here because of circumstances out of her control. That makes me sad, but I know she is so happy that you and I are here together. I look forward to telling her stories about our experiences. It's like Duane made her dream come true through me."

"Oh Mom, I am so glad to be here with you

too," she said, giving me a hug. Alana and I looked down into Dingle Harbor. It was breathtakingly beautiful. Clouds hovered over the bay, but shafts of sunlight found their way through the cracks in the clouds and shone like spotlights on the steel-blue water. I felt as though I had been at this place before, long ago, perhaps in another life. Or was it a memory passed on to me from my ancestors? I will never forget that day and the impression it made upon me. It was a magical moment. My daughter, too, felt the significance of sharing this precious time together.

We drove down the mountain slowly, savoring the lovely scene before us. As we came into town, we noticed there were few people around. We parked near the docks and saw only one other car there. It was a chilly day in Dingle, about 45 degrees. I was wearing a Navy pea coat that I had purchased from an Army surplus store years ago. Made of wool with flannel pockets, it kept me warm. Alana, too, had on a warm wool coat and scarf. We walked around the town slowly, sauntering up and down the narrow, hilly streets. The shops were built in the Georgian style and were painted in bright blues, reds, and greens. We went into the cute shops which sold beautiful ceramic pottery, lace, and jewelry. Alana bought a plaid scarf that was colored moss green and burgundy wine. There were so many colorful scarves; I wanted to buy them all. We stopped at a coffee shop and got a cup of hot chocolate to warm us up. It was the richest cocoa I had ever had; thick and topped with real whipped cream.

"Why is it so quiet in town?" I asked the shopkeeper.

"We're verry busy in summertime. This is Christmas week. People are home cookin' and gettin' ready for thur families to come over."

We thanked her and walked around a bit more, heading for the docks. A very old, rusty fishing boat was tied to the pier, and Alana and I took pictures in front of it. Somewhere there is a wonderful photo of me, looking like a sailor in my Navy pea coat, with the wind blowing through my hair. (Unfortunately, all the photos I took of Ireland were lost when being transferred to an external hard drive.) I took pictures of Alana sitting on a statue of a bronze dolphin, named Fungie. A plaque at the statue's base told his story. He swims into the harbor and follows alongside people in their boats. Fungie is so well loved that the townspeople commissioned the statue in his honor. Dolphins live to be about twenty-five years old, but Fungie is thought to be close to 40. I believe he is still alive and continues to prefer human companionship to that of his own kind.

We left Dingle and drove about one-third of the way around the Ring of Kerry, a total of 110 miles. We drove through the town of Killorglin and stopped along the coast to enjoy the beautiful views of the sea and countryside. We went on a short hike down to the Atlantic Ocean. We stood there for quite some time to watch and listen to the huge waves roll and crash. When we were finally satisfied, we got into our car and headed back to Tralee.

We returned to Tralee in the late afternoon. It was heartwarming to see so many cheerful red-cheeked people walking up and down the streets of the town shopping for their last-minute gifts on the eve of Christmas Eve. Alana and I enjoyed the bustle of the town with its lovely decorations and twinkling lights strung on the old buildings. The main shopping street in Tralee is called Denny Street, which was built in 1826 in Georgian-style architecture. While strolling down Denny Street, I was shocked to see a huge department store called Heaton's. I couldn't believe my eyes.

"Alana, look," I cried out. "There is a store called Heaton's in Ireland, but Heaton is an English name. I have to go in there and buy something." So, we walked into the store and looked around. It was similar to a Target; it had a little of everything. I bought a few toiletries.

"I'm visiting from California and my last name is Heaton. I had to come in here and buy something," I said to the cashier.

"Thank you," he said and nodded politely. He probably thought I was a nut, but I didn't care. I was tickled and couldn't wait to tell Duane that there was a store named after him. Now, I had a brown paper bag with his last name on it to prove it.

CHAPTER 6
Doolin

I LEFT THE DEPARTMENT STORE with a smile on my face and a brown paper bag in my hand, the name "Heaton's" printed in purple ink on the side of the bag. I was getting hungry, so we ventured out to find a good place to eat. Alana had a hankering for fish and chips, which is a very popular dish in Ireland. We found a nice place and ordered our meals. I was eager to get back to the B&B before dark. When we came out of the restaurant, it was twilight. The remaining pink blush of the setting sun was barely visible in the clear night sky.

The inn was several miles away from town, and I did my best to navigate back. I had a difficult time identifying familiar landmarks. To add to my dilemma, darkness had come quickly, and there were no streetlights on the country roads. I made a few wrong turns. I was getting frustrated and so was Alana. It was the first and only time she raised her voice to me during our trip. She yelled, "Mom, don't you know where you are going?"

"Alana, it is very hard for me to drive in the dark, especially in a place where I am not familiar. I need your help to look for street names."

After my plea for assistance, she seemed to calm down. Within a few minutes, we were back at the B&B safe and sound. When we entered the formal parlor, a peat fire burned in the fireplace. The earthy smell was somehow familiar and comforting, and the warmth of the flames felt cozy and inviting. We sat on a floral-patterned, overstuffed couch located in front of the hearth and chatted about our lovely day. Soon we began to feel drowsy and went off to bed.

The next day, Alana and I said our goodbyes and thank yous to Colleen after eating our "light" breakfast of porridge. We left for Doolin, a town on the West Coast. Driving about an hour under overcast skies, we arrived at a ferry crossing in the village of Tarbert. We waited in line for thirty minutes before it was our turn to drive onto the small, flat ferry. The boat could hold ten cars. We crossed a very calm River Shannon.

We landed in Kilrush, a seaside tourist town

with a beach that was completely deserted. The sun finally broke through the clouds as Alana and I got out of our car. We walked towards the shore, admiring the vacant golden sand. The beach was very wide and deep and could accommodate many people. The water was shallow for a long way out. I imagined hundreds of sunburned Irish people on holiday enjoying the beach, playing in the water, and making sandcastles.

Alana and I found a lone open restaurant and ordered soup and brown bread, which, as always, was delicious. There were only a few people inside. It was Christmas Eve, and it felt very strange being so far away from home. I was feeling homesick for my husband and sons, especially being away from them this time of year. We finished our lunch and headed out.

Driving along the West Coast of Ireland was similar to driving on Highway 1 on the coast of California. My spirits began to lift with the sense of familiarity. The sun shone on the Atlantic Ocean, reflecting the sparkling cerulean sky. The air smelled briny, and the seagulls cried out to one another, their white and gray wings flapping in the breeze.

We arrived in Doolin, a little village with a church, a pub, and a few small stores. Its claim to fame was its gorgeous view of the ocean. It didn't disappoint. In addition, Doolin had the reputation for having an active musical scene.

We found our next B&B off a dirt road. When we went to knock on the door, we found a note that said, "Hi Mary and Alana, I will be back at four o'clock. Yvonne." So we decided to drive around the area and found a very old cemetery. We spent a long time looking at the headstones. They were weathered and covered with green lichen; we could barely read the epitaphs. Some of the stones were listing, like drunken soldiers, ready to fall over at any second. The headstones were carved into different shapes. Several were Celtic crosses, others were obelisks, and some were the more common style having straight sides and curved tops. Both Alana and I love the historical significance of cemeteries and visit them wherever we go.

It was about 4:30 p.m. when we headed back to the B&B. We knocked on the door. This time a lovely young woman who said warmly, "My name is Yvonne," greeted us. Yu mus' be Mary and Alana. It's nice to see yur face after talkin' on the phone a few times." She had long blonde hair, a beautiful face, and cornflower blue eyes. She showed us around the inn and explained the rules. A wall photo of Yvonne pictured her being crowned the "Irish Rose" in a beauty pageant.

"Wow—you were the Irish Rose. What an honor."

"Oh, yeah," she said bashfully, "I also teach Irish at the local school." The inn was very new, no more than five years old. The floors and ceilings were made of knotty pine. It was quite cute and comfortable. We were given a room with two twin beds, which suited us perfectly.

Yvonne said to us, "If ya want to go to Mass 'tis at six o'clock. Yu should get thur early 'cause 'tis goin' to be crowded. Ya see, the children are doin' the Nativity. Or yu cun go to regular Christmas Mass tamarra mornin'.""

We thanked her and hurriedly went to get dressed for the evening Mass. It was dark when we arrived at the church. Yvonne had been right; a long line of cars snaked along the roadside. The chapel was called Church of the Holy Rosary, the first Catholic Church so named I had ever heard. Most churches in the States are named after saints. We entered the sanctuary. It was standing room only, so Alana and I stood against the East wall of the church. The chapel was simple and less ornate than other Catholic houses of worship. The walls were whitewashed stucco with an open-beam ceiling constructed of large wooden timbers. Viewing the altar, we saw a bustle of activity. Many children were dressed in costumes for the Nativity Mass.

The priest walked up to the podium and said,

"Good evenin' folks. I'm Father O'Malley, fur those of yu tha' don't know me. Tonight yur in fur a treat. The children here, ages five tu twelve are goin' tu do the Mass. I don' need tu say another word." He walked off the altar. And so began the most beautiful Mass I had ever witnessed. The pure innocence of the children telling the story of the birth of Jesus in their sweet, lilting, Irish brogues was captivating. The children looked adorable wearing their long robes, headdresses of blue and white, and little sandals on their small feet.

A few live sheep stood by the young shepherds; a live donkey by Mary and Joseph. A boy of about eight years began to speak. Narrating the first act of the play, he spoke in the most angelic voice.

"And thur were, in the same country, shepherds, abiding in thu fields, keeping watch over their flocks, by night. And lo, thu angel of thu Lord came upon them and thu glory of thu Lord shown roun' about them and they were sore afraid. The angel said, Fear not, for behold, I bring yu tidings of great joy that should be to all people. For unto yu, born this day, in the City of David, a Savior, 'tis Christ thu Lord. And this will be a sign unto yu. Yu will find a babe wrapped in swaddling clothes, lying in a manger. And suddenly, thur was with thu angels a multitude of thu heavenly host, praising God and saying, Glory to God in thu highest and on earth, peace and goodwill towards men.'"

And so began the play. Alana and I looked at each other. With tears running down our cheeks, we smiled at each other. Without words, we knew this was the most memorable Christmas Eve ever.

CHAPTER 7
Cliffs of Moher

L EAVING THE SERVICE ON CHRISTMAS Eve, I felt Alana and I were unquestionably meant to be in Ireland. Children always open ours eyes and ears to what is truly important. I had struggled with the idea of going to Europe without my husband because of his illness, but his selflessness showed me the true meaning of Christmas.

Alana and I drove back to the inn and slept peacefully that night. Yvonne had told us that she had searched a thirty-mile radius to find a restaurant that would be open on Christmas Day. The only place open, The Falls River Hotel, was fifteen miles away in the town of Ennistymon. Yvonne had taken the liberty of making a reservation for us.

We woke up Christmas morning in our cozy beds and said "Merry Christmas" to each other. Yvonne had a girl from town make us breakfast.

We could hear Yvonne and her family celebrating Christmas behind the door that was marked "Private" at the inn.

After breakfast, Alana and I planned to visit the Cliffs of Moher. They are known worldwide and are a popular tourist destination. Yvonne warned us, "Now don' yu be climbin' o'er the fence. Mind tha' yu stay away from the edge. A tourist last week was blown off a cliff and fell to her death when a big gust of wind pushed her off."

"Don't worry Yvonne, I am afraid of heights. There is no way I am going to be near the edge of the cliff, and I won't let Alana either."

We thanked her for the advice and got into our car. It was a very brisk, overcast day. We wore our wool coats, hats, and scarves to fight off the Irish chill. The cliffs were about ten miles away, so it didn't take us long to get there. A few other families were walking on the trail by the cliffs. I could hear them speaking different languages: Spanish, German, and Italian. Alana and I hadn't come across any Americans yet, which was very unusual.

While walking along the asphalt pathway to the cliffs, I was glad the wind was mild. I didn't want to witness any mishaps. Alana and I came up to the wooden fence and admired the view of the ocean. The sea was calm that morning. We could see gulls flying above the water, cawing to one another. We also noticed a unique bird called the Atlantic Puffin, which has a very colorful beak of orange and red. Its body is black and white, and its face is snow white with coal black eyes. It was fun to watch them on the water bobbing up and down.

The cliffs were sheer vertical drops down to the ocean. There was no beach. We could hear the waves crashing against the rocks below. If we looked either left or right, we could see the other cliffs, standing like sentinels along the coast. We were able to gauge the cliffs at about 400 feet in height from the ocean to the top. In some spots, they rose as high as 700 feet above the water.

"Wow. I wouldn't want to be blown off one of those," I said to Alana. We could see a few people who had climbed over the fence and were getting close to the edge. I couldn't look at them; it made me nervous. When we finished admiring the rugged coastline, we got into our car and headed toward the Falls River Hotel for our Christmas dinner. I drove through many little villages dotted with whitewashed cottages and fields of kelly green grass. Hedgerows separated the farmers' lands from one another and the roads. From the distance, the land looked like an antique crazy patchwork quilt.

When we came upon the town of Ennistymon, there was a scattering of houses on either side of the road. The town was lovely, with the Inagh River cascading down in waterfalls along the roadside. The Falls River Hotel is a commanding building, with gabled dormers running across the upper story of the structure. Erected in the 1700s, the original house was built of old, bumpy gray stones. The other wings of the hotel were added on over time. Alana and I walked up the grand stone staircase to the hotel and turned around to see a wonderful view of the gorgeous cascades. Lush green vegetation lined the riverbank. It was quite the picture postcard scene.

We waited in the formal lobby to be seated. The Maître d' escorted us to our table, pulled out our chairs, and placed white linen napkins on our laps. The menu had three choices each of appetizers, entrees, and desserts. No prices were listed on the menu; prix fixe was printed on the bottom. I realized this was one fancy restaurant. The dining room was lovely. The huge twelve-foot tall windows let us view the beautiful grounds. Our chairs were heavy and well made. The carpet was very plush, burgundy in color, with a golden circular pattern throughout.

Alana ordered soup and the, Duck á l'Orange and I ordered a salad and the rib-eye steak. We both ordered the fig pudding because we never had it before and it sounded very Old World. While enjoying our food, I noticed that the restaurant was quite busy. Large groups of people were celebrating together as well as tables with couples quietly dining. The service was leisurely to allow us time to savor our food and converse. This was a switch for two Americans who are used to fast service and eating quickly. For once, I was trying not to be in a hurry. What for? We have nowhere else to be, I thought to myself. We ate our "figgy pudding" and found it to be mediocre.

We had been waiting for the check for a long time. After about twenty minutes, I looked for someone to help us. I finally went out to the front desk and told them I wanted to pay my bill. The gentleman asked, "Are yu stayin' at the hotel, Ladies?"

"No, we just came to have dinner," I said.

"Well then, that will be 200 Euros, please."

"200 Euros. Are you sure that's right?" I blurted out.

"That is correct Madam," the Maître d' said curtly.

I pulled out my credit card and handed it to him with hesitation. I was very angry to have paid so much for a meal. I had never in my life paid that much at a restaurant. A dinner at San Francisco's most elegant restaurant didn't cost that much money. Oh well, there was nothing I could do about it. After all, we were having Christmas dinner in Ireland.

The next morning when we were saying goodbye to Yvonne, I debated whether or not to tell her about the cost of our food the night before. I decided to go ahead and tell her. I said as delicately as I could, "Yvonne, I just wanted to let you know that we had a nice dinner at the Falls River Hotel, but it was extremely expensive—200 Euros."

"That's abou' right for a Christmas dinner at that hotel."

"Well, you may want to warn your patrons before you make a reservation for them in the future. They may not want to pay that much money."

"Well, 'twas the only place open. Mind yu, thur was no choice," she said defensively. I learned my lesson: Always ask what they fixed the prices at when there is a prix-fixe menu.

CHAPTER 8
Oughterard

I T WAS A GLORIOUSLY SUNNY day in Ireland on December 26, very unusual for that time of year. Alana and I enjoyed the sights as we drove along the coast watching the subtle swell of the ocean. The sea birds were diving into the water to catch fish. Yvonne told us we must stop at Burren National Park, just a few miles up the road. She told us it was on our way to Oughterard, our next stop, and was an historical landmark that we must see. As we drove several miles north, the land began to change. The rocks became flat and had long cracks, called "grikes," crisscrossing them. We pulled to the side of the road and parked our car. We read the park sign to get information about what we were seeing. The rock was limestone called "karst." It had been covered by glacial ice only

100,000 years before, quite recent by geologic standards. Grass and flowers grew between the fissures of the rock. It was quite pleasing to the eye, and all I could think of was they were like natural paving stones with vegetation growing between them.

This area also held archaeological sites where ancient people used the stones to make tombs for their dead thousands of years ago. Ninety megalithic tombs are present over the landscape of many square miles of karst. The ancient people would somehow pry up the flat stones and make walls and a roof to make an enclosure for a body. I was in awe of the age of this land and its people, and the fact that they were my ancestors.

We continued our journey and were planning to stop in Galway where some of my relatives came from, but when we got there, it was like a ghost town. We drove down a main street of the city of 75,000 people and no one was about; the shops were all closed. Because we couldn't get into any buildings, we decided to keep going. I was disappointed because I had heard it was a nice place to visit. Galway was situated near the ocean, but the road to Oughterard brought us inland.

The terrain changed yet again from a flat appearance to hills of viridian green and small groves of forest pine. Marshes full of tulle and cattails surrounded the narrow country road. The marshes housed egrets, ducks and smaller songbirds. The hills began to grow in size and became ancient mountains, which were eroded for thousands of years by constant rain. The environment had a magical quality, and we could see why stories had been made up about fairies and leprechauns.

After a few hours of driving through the beautiful countryside, we came upon Oughterard, a small town of 1,300 souls. The Owenriff River flows around the town and contains a lovely old stone bridge called The Quiet Man Bridge. It was named after the movie of that same name, starring John Wayne and Maureen O'Hara, in the 1950s. Not far away is Lough (Lake) Corrib, a favorite local fishing spot that brings in anglers from all over Ireland.

We quickly located The Boat Inn where we were staying for the evening, and parked our car in front of it. Alana and I strolled through the village looking in the few shops that were open and decided to head back to the inn because we were getting hungry. Most inns in Ireland also have pubs in them, which is very convenient for the weary traveler.

Alana and I ordered our soup of the day and brown bread once again. What can I say? It was cheap and always delicious. The pub looked pretty typical of ones in Ireland; dark wood and cozy and not much light. We finished our food and noticed that more and more people started coming into the place. And not only that, but the woman were dressed to the nines in fancy outfits of satins, silks and lace.

I asked our waitress, "What's going on? Why are all the women so dressed up? Is there going to be a party tonight?"

"Well, sort of. 'Tis St. Stephen's Day, don't yu know.

"I never heard of St. Stephen's Day. What does it commemorate?"

"Well, I'm not sure, but the people in Ireland celebrate more this day, than even New Year's Eve. It's goin' tu git crazy here in a few hours."

We thanked her for the information and left the restaurant feeling very out of place in our jeans and plain shirts, so we went up to our room. We were tired anyway and wanted to go to bed early. Our room was very basic, with two twin beds, a nightstand and lamp. Everything was a bit worn. Alana had found the inn online and chose it because it was inexpensive. Oh well, at least the room had its own bathroom.

Alana and I went to sleep. A few hours later, I heard yelling from the hallway outside our room. I sat up abruptly and was scared. I listened for a while, so that maybe I could hear what was going on. The walls of the inn were paper-thin and I heard what was being said.

A young woman was crying and was saying to young man, "Why were you looking at her like that?"

"What is yu talkin' about? I wasn't lookin' at her."

"Yu were too. Just leave. I don' want to talk to yu anymore," she yelled.

"Aw, why da yu have to be such a bitch?" he yelled and slammed the door.

I don't know how Alana was sleeping through all of this. I could also hear people outside yelling and laughing. I thought, what the hell is going on? Then I remembered what the waitress told us and realized that the people were getting out of hand because of all the drinking and partying for St. Stephen's Day.

The young man came back, banging on the door next to our room, yelling, "Come on Fiona. Don' be like that. Let me in, pleeze."

Alana woke up with that racket. She said sleepily, "What's going on, Mom?"

"The locals are really partying and it's getting ridiculous. We are never going to be able to get to sleep with all this noise." We lay there and listened to people yelling, bottles breaking, and doors slamming. I said to Alana, "Thank God we are only staying here one night."

"Don't blame me, Mom, I didn't know about St. Stephen's Day when I booked the room," she said in her defense. We finally fell asleep around three in the morning.

We showered and dressed slowly from lack of sleep. When we entered the pub for breakfast, we couldn't believe our eyes. Hundreds of beer bottles and glasses littered every table and the bar. We found a table with the least amount of debris on it. The waitress came over and apologized for the mess, "I am so sorry. I didn't get out of here 'til four this mornin' and I had to come back after a few hours sleep."

"What happened in here last night? We heard so much yelling and commotion."

"Well, a few fights broke out and me boss over thur had to kick everyone out of the pub. So all the people just kept celebratin' outside," she said defeatedly.

"You poor thing. You must be exhausted," I said sympathetically.

The Twelve Bens—Connemara National Park

Kylemore Abbey

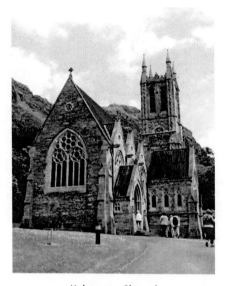

Kylemore Chapel

The Nun's Cemetery

Sister Conroy's headstone

Clonmacnoise Castle ruins

O'Rourke Tower at Clonmacnoise

McCarthy's Tower at Clonmacnoise

Claffey headstone

McDermott Cathedral and MacClaffey's Church

Claffey headstone at Clonmacnoise

MacClaffey's Church

Claffey headstone

River Liffy, Dublin

Fusilier's Arch

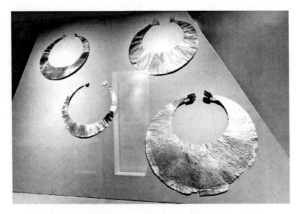

Gold collars, Museum of Natural History, Dublin

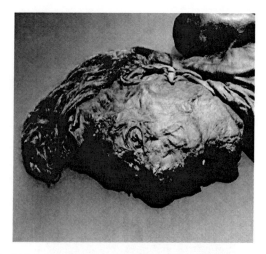

Head of Clonycavan Man, Museum of Natural History, Dublin

Stained glass windows at St. Patrick's Cathedral, Dublin

St. Patrick's Cathedral, Dublin

Alana and Mary

CHAPTER 9
The Boat Inn

I LOOKED AT THE YOUNG serving woman closely. She was lovely with strawberry-blonde hair, spring green eyes, and a milky complexion. We ordered porridge for breakfast and she left us. She went about the pub collecting beer bottles and glasses, working quickly. She balanced the glassware expertly on her tray, swiftly walking to the back of the bar where she placed the glasses carefully in the sink with soapy water and with a loud crash, dumped the bottles in the trash bin.

The owner of the pub was behind the bar washing glasses as fast as his employee could bring them. I couldn't help but notice him; he was a doppelganger for Gabriel Byrne, one of my favorite actors. He had a head of wavy black hair, piercing blue eyes and high cheekbones. He was not tall, but built like a heavyweight boxer with broad shoulders. He sure looked like he could kick anyone out of the pub with ease.

I saw the waitress quietly chatting with him as she unloaded her burden. He then looked over at us with concern on his face. He dried his hands on a cotton dishtowel that hung from a hook on the back wall. I began to feel a bit nervous as he strode over to where we were sitting. He stood before us, as handsome as could be, and I was speechless. He said in a deep baritone voice, "Ladies, I want tu make my apologies for last night. Fiona over there told me you didn't sleep a wink 'cause of all the racket."

I was startled as I looked over at the girl, Fiona. Could she be the same Fiona I heard last night? I thought to myself.

And after what seemed like an eternity, I sputtered out, "That's okay. It's not your fault. The people were just celebrating and having a good time. When people drink too much there is bound to be some trouble. She told us you kicked them all out of the bar. That must have been something to see."

"Ah, 'twas no trouble. But I feel terrible. I want tu give yu yur breakfast free, tu make up fur it. I don' want yu to have a bad opinion of the place."

"Aw, that is very kind of you sir."

"Where yu Ladies from, may I ask?"

"We're from California, a town called Livermore, not far from San Francisco."

"Oh, I always wanted to go to San Francisco. Maybe one day," he said.

"Oh, you must go. It is a wonderful place to visit," I said with enthusiasm. "May I ask you a favor? Can you please tell us about St. Stephen's Day? Do you know the history?"

"Sure. My da would tell me stories about it when I wuz a lad. St. Stephen was the first Christian martyr. It was said that after our Lord's crucifixion, St. Stephen was hidin' from the Roman soldiers when a wren chirped, givin' away his hidin' place, and the men stoned him to death for bein' a Christian. So, on St. Stephen's Day, children used tu go 'round stoning wrens to reenact what tuk place years ago. The children would tie the dead wren to a stick and go 'round asking fur money so that they could have a dance for the village to celebrate. They call 'em Wren Boys. They blacken thur faces and wear tall straw hats and dance and sing fur people. Thur are only a few places left in Ireland where they do that now. Mostly, people celebrate by drinkin'."

"Thank you for taking the time to talk with us," I said.

"Well, Ladies, I mus' get back tu work. It was

nice meetin' yu. Safe journey."

"Nice meeting you, too, and thank you for being so kind to my daughter and me." Before we knew it, Fiona brought us our bowls of steaming hot porridge. We thanked her and she was off in a flash, cleaning up more bottles. "Alana, I wonder if that is the Fiona I heard arguing with her boyfriend last night?" I said with concern.

"Who knows, Mom? Fiona is a common name in Ireland."

"Well, let's go up and pack our things. We have a long day ahead of us."

We thanked Fiona once again and I gave her a nice tip. Maybe that would cheer her up after the horrendous night she had. Alana and I went upstairs and spread out the map of Ireland on the bed to confirm where we were going that day. Heading northwest to Connemara, our first stop would be Kylemore Abbey, a beautiful manor house. Then, we were going to Connemara State Park for a hike. Lastly, we were going to end up spending the night at Abbeyglen Castle. I couldn't wait. Any place had to be better than The Boat Inn on St. Stephen's Day.

CHAPTER 10
Connemara

T HE DAY WAS GRAY AND drizzly as we headed out to Kylemore Abbey on the West Coast of Ireland. Alana had found it on the Internet while she was researching interesting places to go on our trip. I had seen a picture and it looked very pleasant, but nothing prepared me for its grandeur.

As we drove up and gazed upon Kylemore Castle, it struck me as one of the most magnificent man-made places I have ever seen. Mitchell Henry, a wealthy English textile manufacturer and politician, bought the property in the 1850s and construction began in 1857. It was to be a gift to his wife, Margaret. It took one hundred men and four years to complete the gorgeous estate. The castle itself is 40,000 square feet and has thirty-three bedrooms, four bathrooms, four sitting rooms, a ballroom, a gunroom, a schoolroom, a smoking room, and a formal Victorian garden. The building is made of limestone and granite from Ireland and spreads out across a lavish green landscape. It is light gray in color, with the edging stone of dark gray granite. The turrets are square, instead of cylindrical, as in a medieval castle.

The Henrys had nine children, but in 1875, Margaret died of a fever while she was visiting Egypt. Mitchell was heartbroken and didn't spend much time at the estate after his wife's death. In 1909, he sold it to the Duke and Duchess of Manchester. And only eleven years later, it was lost to the Duke and Duchess because of their gambling debts.

Adjacent to the main house is a Benedictine Abbey. The original abbey was in Belgium but was bombed during World War I. The nuns were looking for a place to build a new abbey and purchased the castle and grounds in 1920. The chapel is a miniature model of the Bristol Cathedral in England and made from green Irish marble. Mitchell, his wife, and a great grandnephew are entombed in a mausoleum at the abbey.

Alana and I walked around the grounds, but unfortunately the building was closed because it was Christmas week in Ireland. It was the one downfall of traveling at this time of year but was still a great place to visit because the setting was so lovely. A lake is situated directly in front of the castle, which is reflected in the still, dark water. A mountain rises across from the lake, and the serenity of the location is beyond belief.

My favorite part of our walk was when we went to the abbey and saw the little cemetery adjacent to it. I have always loved cemeteries, ever since I was a little girl. I believe it has to do with the history of them and the peacefulness of the grounds. The headstones were in neat rows of ten and very plain. They were typical, arched on top and flat sided. The best part was reading the names of the nuns and the ages they were when they died. I noticed most of them lived into their eighties and nineties. Here were some of the names: Sister Mary Margaret, born 1852, died 1948, aged 94 years; Sister Margaret Frances, born 1865, died 1953, aged 82 years; Sister M. Dymphina Conroy, born 1904, died 2006, aged 102 years.

I thought, maybe I should have given my life to God and I could have lived in a gorgeous place like this and lived a long life because having a husband and five children really does bring a lot of stress to my life.

I said to Alana, "I guess there are perks to being a nun after all. Maybe a life of poverty, chastity, and obedience wouldn't be so bad."

"Oh, Mom. There is no way you could live the life of a nun. You love your husband and kids too much, especially me." she smiled.

"Oh, I know Alana. I can't imagine my life without being a Mom. Even though it gets really hard, I wouldn't want it any other way—the stress, challenges and all that goes with it. It's not how long you live. It's the quality of your life that really matters."

"I completely agree, Mom. Just like this place. It is so beautiful, but could you really live here all the time? It is so quiet."

"Yes, it could get a little lonesome out here, but what fun it would be if you carted in loads of family and friends to share it with."

Our next stop, Connemara National Park, actually encompasses the Kylemore Estate and the surrounding area, so we didn't have to drive far to the park headquarters. It has several trails to choose from to take a hike and we chose the easiest. In the distance I could clearly see Diamond Hill, so named for its diamond-shaped pointy top. It is 1460 feet in elevation, and if Alana and I had been more energetic, we may have hiked to the summit, but it takes two to three hours to climb, and we were looking forward to getting to Abbeyglen Castle in the early afternoon since we were only staying one night.

So, we hiked halfway up Diamond Hill and had a breathtaking view of the Atlantic Ocean in the distance and the luscious marshland and sparkling delta spreading out on the horizon. The wind was blowing the briny scent into our heaving lungs, and it felt wonderful to be alive and in Ireland. After we soaked in the magnificent view, we descended the hill carefully and headed to our hotel, which was less than twenty miles away, thank goodness.

We drove leisurely to the town of Clifden and found Sky Road, which led us to Abbeyglen Castle. We came upon the inn and found it to be very picturesque. Abbeyglen Castle was about a third the size of Kylemore Castle, but lovely just the same. It was set up on a small hill with a sloping expanse of bright green manicured lawn in the front of the building. It looked to be three stories tall and spread out, and was really a manor house more than it was a castle.

We went into the formal lobby, which was all done in mahogany and quite grand. Our room had a huge canopied bed that looked fit for a queen. I was in awe and loving every moment of the extravagance compared to our plain room at the Boat Inn. Our room looked out to the beautiful lawn, and I was content.

We then went out to explore the hotel. I found a payphone in the lobby and told Alana that I wanted to call Duane because it had been a few days since I had spoken to him. The phone was hung on the wall and across from it was a huge silver cage. In the cage was a huge African gray parrot with a strong black beak that looked as though it could snap off a finger.

I smiled at the parrot as I made my call to Duane. And when I heard the phone pick up I said, "Hello, Duane. It's me."

"Hi Mary, so good to hear from you," he said excitedly.

"Hello, woo-hoo," said the parrot very loudly.

"Mary, who's that? What's going on?" Duane asked suspiciously.

"Duane, nobody is with me. That is a parrot you are hearing." I laughed.

"Woo-hoo. Hi baby," the parrot squawked.

"Mary, really, that's a parrot? It sure sounds like a guy to me."

"Duane, seriously, you have got to believe me. It's a huge, gray parrot. I guess the hotel management thought it would be funny to put a parrot next to the payphone."

CHAPTER 11
Gilbert and Abbeyglen Castle

AFTER MY PHONE CALL TO Duane, Alana and I began our tour of Abbeyglen Castle. We walked to the reception desk to ask the concierge about the precocious parrot. "Excuse me, sir. Can you please tell me the name of the huge gray parrot by the pay phone?"

"Yes, Madam. 'Is name's Gilbert," he said with a smile.

"Thank you. I guess I expected something a little more Irish," I said, sounding a bit disappointed.

"The owners named 'im after thu famous Irish musician, Gilbert O'Sullivan."

"I am not familiar with that name. What song is he famous for?'

"Do yu recall a song, 'Alone Again, Naturally,'

from the seventies?"

"I sure do. I still don't think Gilbert is an Irish first name."

"Oh, 'tisn't really. Gilbert O'Sullivan's first name was actually Raymond, but he changed it tu Gilbert. A play on the musical team, Gilbert and Sullivan."

"Oh, that was clever of him. How old is Gilbert? The parrot I mean?"

"'E's 15, I'm thinkin'."

"Wow, Gilbert can sure say a lot of words for a fifteen-year old bird. Thanks for telling me about Gilbert. I believe my daughter and I will explore the hotel a bit."

Suddenly, I heard a whooshing noise. Gilbert had landed on the counter and was waddling across the reception desk. He strutted over to the call bell and pecked at it, dinging it several times and saying, "First name, last name, please."

This intelligent bird astonished us. We laughed so hard. Gilbert was definitely a hit with us at this hotel. "Goodbye, Gilbert," we said in unison.

"Goodbye, Ladies," Gilbert said with gusto.

We wandered down the hall and found a pub within the building. At one time, it appears to have been a gentlemen's smoking room. There was a definite masculine feel to the room with its leather chairs, burgundy and hunter green plush carpeting, and dark mahogany trim. We ordered gin and tonics and pretended to be cousins visiting their wealthy relatives. The window provided us with a lovely view of the lawn and gardens. After our hike, it was quite relaxing to sit and enjoy the beautiful surroundings. We continued our explorations.

We walked the grounds and down the sloping green lawn. The sun had finally shown itself through the clouds, and we relished the warmth. The mountains surrounding the hotel were called the Twelve Bens. They are twelve pointy-topped mountains, one after another, all in a row that looks like pins. Bens is the Irish word for pins, hence the name Twelve Bens. The full Gaelic Irish name of the range is Na Beanna Beola.

I looked back at Abbeyglen Castle sitting regally upon on the hill. A man named John D'Arcy had it built in 1832 and named it Glenowen. He was a wealthy man who had built Clifden Castle back in 1815. He wanted to improve the area, so he founded the town of Clifden. For a while, the manor house was leased to a parish priest. The Irish Mission Society bought it in 1854 and used it as an orphanage for protestant girls being trained as domestic servants.

In 1953 it became a coed orphanage and was supported by local patrons. It closed in 1955 due to lack of funds. The building fell derelict and became home to sheep and cattle for some time.

In the 1960s, Mr. Padraig Joyce and his wife of Clifden purchased the house. They ran Glenowen until 1969 when the Hughes family took over. It was renamed Abbeyglen Castle and soon became one of Connemara's most prestigious hotels.

We were getting hungry. We needed to dress for dinner, so we trudged back up the hill to the hotel. We had each packed one fancy dress for such occasions. Luckily, no one was going to see us two nights in a row. Our party frocks made several appearances as we trekked across Ireland. As we headed towards the dining room, we kept a lookout for Gilbert, but he was nowhere to be found.

Entering the dining room, I honestly felt as though I were in a castle. The room was elegantly furnished. The many crystal chandeliers sparkled in the dim light. Several tall windows were dressed with curtains of thick brocade and striped fabric of burgundy, navy, and hunter green. The walls were painted the color of Syrah wine, and the tables were covered with starched white linen. The china plates and silverware shined in the candlelight. It was the most romantic dining room I had ever seen. I was truly missing Duane and desperately wished that he were here to share this lovely experience with me.

Alana and I had a wonderful meal together. The service was impeccable. We appreciated the elegance of the restaurant compared to the many other places we had eaten in Ireland. I felt as though I went back in time to the early 1900s. What a strange and wonderful feeling.

After our fantastic meal, we headed off to bed in our regal room with the four poster-canopied bed. Alana slept in the twin bed on the other side of the room. Even though I offered to share the big bed with her, she declined. As I lay in my massive bed, I felt so lonely for my husband. I was thinking of him and his fragile health. I prayed that all would be well. Finally, sleep came.

I woke the next morning, refreshed and ready for the long day ahead. It was a two-hour ride to the city of Athlone—a long drive by my standards. Smack dab in the center of Ireland, Athlone is where my ancestors, the Claffey's, emigrated from 150 years earlier. I couldn't wait to see what the day had in store for us.

CHAPTER 12
Athlone

IT WAS DECEMBER 28, AND we were at the tail end of our trip. We were headed to the city of Athlone in the middle of Ireland, or midlands, as the Irish call it. My great, great grandfather Peter Claffey, born in 1841, came from Offaly County near Athlone.

So, with map in hand, Alana and I we were on our way. While driving along the country road, we were stopped by a flock of sheep. Alana and I found it quite amusing as we sat patiently waiting for the farmer to herd them onto the next road. The sheep wore their full winter wool coats. Their lambs had filled out and no longer resembled spindly newborns. We watched as mothers nudged their young along in front of them, baaing constantly.

As we got closer to Athlone, we glimpsed many houses along the roadside. Once in the city, we could see the mighty River Shannon in the distance. The wide and swiftly moving Shannon would test the abilities of even the strongest swimmers. I didn't intend to take that challenge.

We drove across Battery Bridge. It was built in 1566 during the ninth year of Queen Elizabeth's reign. Made of stone with nine arches, the bridge was 360 feet long and 14 feet wide. It was rebuilt in 1844. In the 1960s, it was overhauled once again when it became too dangerous to allow car traffic. We parked our car on the cobblestone street near Athlone Castle. We walked around the structure to find the front opening, but it was closed for the day. On the small side for a castle, it was made with immense blocks of limestone and seemed impenetrable. Athlone Castle wasn't a fancy fairytale castle; it was a fortress made for battle and protection.

On a side street we found our lodging, the Bastion Inn. Sandwiched between two other businesses, the inn was painted bright colors of sky blue, fuchsia, and red. You couldn't miss it. When we entered, we immediately fell in love with the B&B. It was very old and had a narrow wooden staircase. Our room had low ceilings with interesting angles. Twin beds with chenille spreads sat under each of the two windows. The windows looked out onto the street below. It was a very cozy place.

We spoke to the innkeeper, Anthony, about nearby restaurants, and he suggested a Thai place around the corner. When we returned to the inn after dinner, we saw a family happily chatting together in the tearoom. We introduced ourselves to one another. They were the only other Americans we had encountered, and we had been in Ireland nine days.

They were the Flood family from Michigan. The parents, Jim and Patti, and their teenage children, Sarah, Aimee, and Michael formed a handsome family. Patti appeared so young that she looked like a sister to her children. She was an attractive brunette with an olive complexion and trim figure. Sarah, the oldest child, was striking. With her almost black hair, brown eyes, and snow-white skin, she looked so much like Alana. Aimee and Michael had their father's dark blond hair and blue eyes.

You could tell they were a loving family by how they interacted with one another. They were trying to figure out where they were going to eat that night, and we told them about the Thai restaurant. Anthony came into the room and said, "Yu all mus' go to Sean's Bar and meet up after dinner. 'Tis a wonderful place and 'tis been around since AD 900."

"It's really that old?" I chimed in.

"It surely is and yu canna miss goin' there."

"That sounds great." said Jim enthusiastically.

"We'll see you there later." So, that evening we walked to Sean's Bar, which was literally around the corner from the Bastion Inn and across from Athlone Castle.

When we entered, I couldn't believe how old the pub looked. The hearth had an ancient appearance. The stone, worn by 1,100 years of peat fires, had a deep depression in it. The wooden bar had many scratches and nicks. The seating area, where the oak bar stools sat, was very narrow. I actually felt as though I had gone back in time.

Alana and I looked around a bit for the Flood family. They hadn't arrived yet, so we each ordered a Guinness. I had never drunk a Guinness beer before. I don't believe Alana had either because she was only nineteen. Arthur Guinness first brewed the dry stout in Dublin in the 1700s. It is quite different from other beers. Coffee-colored, the beer has a thick consistency and a nutty flavor—very tasty.

While we were sitting in the pub, more people began to trickle in. In the corner by the front door, we saw three people taking out musical instruments. One person had an acoustic guitar; another, a tin whistle; and the third, a hand drum. The drum, known as a Bodhran (pronounced Bough-rawn), looks like a large tambourine without the encircling cymbals. The surface of the drum is usually made from goatskin stretched taut over a circular wooden ring about two inches in circumference. A wooden tipper is used to strike the drum. The Bodhran is very popular in Irish music today and was introduced in the early twentieth century.

The musicians began to play some Irish tunes I was not familiar with. Soon, they played some American music. As in all Irish pubs, everyone is encouraged to sing along. I went over, sat down with them, and sang my heart out. We sang "Country Roads"; "California Dreamin'"; and "Hotel California"—the last two songs in honor of Alana and me, the California natives. This experience was quite thrilling for me—singing in an Irish pub.

The Floods finally arrived, and we ordered another Guinness. We took our drinks into the beer garden that was in back of the pub. It was a huge room, sixty feet by sixty feet, and boasted a retractable ceiling that closed in case of rain or extreme cold. It was marvelous.

Alana and Sarah, both of legal drinking age,

were enjoying themselves and the beer garden. The younger teenagers, Michael and Aimee, were feeling a bit out of their element in the pub so their mom walked them back to the inn. Meanwhile, I chatted with Jim in the beer garden.

As we were chatting, a man walked up to us and introduced himself as Tom. "I heard you both talkin' with American accents, so I had to cum over. I used tu live in thu States."

"Hi Tom, I'm Mary. I live near San Francisco. Where did you live?"

"I lived in Ohio with my wife. She is an American, but we got divorced. I lived in the U.S. for twenty-five years. After we split up, I came back to Ireland, but I still miss living thur and when I hear someone with an American accent, I like tu chat with them."

"Hi, Tom. My name is Jim and I'm from Michigan." Jim held out his hand and shook Tom's. "I am here with my wife Patti and our three kids."

Tom said to me, "Are yu here with anyone, Mary?"

"Yes, I'm here with my daughter, Alana. She's over there, talking with Jim's oldest daughter, Sarah."

"Where is yur husband?" Tom asked curiously.

"Oh, he is at home. He gave me a trip to Ireland for a Christmas gift."

Tom and Jim both looked at me strangely. And then Tom said hesitantly, "Why would a man be lettin' his wife and daughter be travelin' alone at Christmas time?"

Since I was having my second Guinness, I had become a bit more open. "Do you really want to know the true reason?"

Jim said, "Yes, I do. I was wondering myself."

"Well, then I'll tell you. My husband has lymphoma. It's a type of cancer. He had chemo a year and a half ago, but the cancer is back. We went to Stanford for a second opinion and the doctor told us that my husband needs to have his spleen removed. So in January he is going to have surgery. He gave me this trip to Ireland because he knew it was a dream of mine. You see, he may not make it through the operation and he knew that I may never get to Ireland because our youngest child, Sam, is nine and I might not ever be able to afford coming over here," I said with tears in my eyes.

Jim and Tom looked at me. Their eyes welled up with tears. They couldn't speak. Then Jim broke the silence by saying, "I am a general physician and it sounds like your husband is getting great care. He is young, and I believe he will make it through the surgery."

"Thanks for saying that, Jim. I really hope so. It was very difficult for me to leave my husband to go on this trip, but he insisted that I go. It was his gift to me. I had to honor him by coming, don't you see?"

Tom finally found the words to speak and said, "Mary, yu got quite a husband there."

"She sure does," Jim added.

Patti had arrived back at the pub and sensed the mood had become a bit somber. I knew that Jim would fill her in later, so I wouldn't have to tell my story again.

At that point, Tom excused himself and took off to find someone else to talk to. Patti said to me, "Mary, what are you doing tomorrow?"

"We are leaving for Dublin. Why?"

"Tomorrow morning we are going to a monastery called Clonmacnoise. It is about ten miles from here. It is supposed to be really amazing. It wouldn't take you too much off course."

"That sounds really great, Patti. Let me talk with Alana about it, and I will let you know. In fact, let me go ask her now."

I walked over and told Alana about the monastery. She thought it was a great idea. Since we were going to have to wake up early the next morning, we decided to head back to the B&B. Jim, Patti, and Sarah also agreed with our plan and followed us back to the Bastion to get some sleep.

CHAPTER 13
Clonmacnoise

W E WOKE UP AT SEVEN o'clock because we wanted to get an early start to Clonmacnoise Monastery. The sky that morning was ominous. Storm clouds looked ready to burst open at any second. We had been lucky; this was our tenth day in Ireland and our first real rainstorm.

We joined our American friends in the tearoom for an early breakfast. We chatted about how much fun we had at Sean's bar the night before. Bags packed, we met outside where our cars were parked on the street. I asked them to drive slowly because I did. Jim said, "Sarah is driving. She doesn't drive fast."

So, off we went on our adventure. The monastery was about twelve miles south of Athlone. I navigated the road's many potholes as the heavy rain descended on us. It was difficult to see where I was going. The windshield wipers were doing their best to rid the glass of the big, fat raindrops. Luckily, no one else was driving at that hour because it was still Christmas week.

Thirty minutes later, we arrived at our destination in a steady downpour. We ran up to the gate to discover a sign that read: Clonmacnoise Monastery opens at 10:00 a.m. It was only eight-thirty. "Oh, darn it," I said with exasperation. "I never thought to call to see what time it opened."

"Well, we didn't either," Patti said apologetically.

"The wall is pretty low. Why don't we just climb over it and we can pay later?" Jim said with a twinkle in his eye.

I watched as the Floods scaled the wall. I don't know what came over me. I almost never break the rules, but that day I said, "The hell with it, I'm going over too." Alana followed suit, breaking into the monastery. It was all very exciting and made me feel alive and adventurous.

Cairan, a young Christian man from the nearby village of Rathcroghan, founded Clonmacnoise in AD 546. The monastery originally consisted of a wooden church and outbuildings on the east bank of the River Shannon. It was a religious center and a site for trade and craftsmanship for centuries. The wooden structures were eventually replaced with stone in the ninth century. The ruins of a cathedral, seven churches, and two high towers can be visited at the site. The cylindrical towers with conical roofs were built to hide the monks and protect the religious artifacts from plunder. The invaders were a persistent lot. The Irish raided the monastery twenty-seven times, the Vikings, seven times, and the Anglo-Normans, six times.

As I walked among the ancient stone buildings, I felt a sense of awe and a connection to this holy place. Positioned on a small, emerald hill, the Cross of the Scriptures, a High Celtic stone cross, stood majestically at thirteen feet tall. I gazed down at the River Shannon as tiny rays of sunlight peeked through the dark clouds. I saw that the water had risen up the banks close to the monastery. *I wonder if the river had ever flooded this place before.* I later learned that in AD 940, the river washed away half the buildings of the monastery.

We strolled in and out of doorless churches and began to walk around the oldest headstones. Unfortunately, the names had been worn down by countless other rainstorms over the millennium, and we could not read them. But as we rambled farther away from the churches, the stones became legible with the names of thousands of souls who had passed before us. On the outermost concentric ring, I found my ancestor's name plainly written upon white marble stone, CLAFFEY. So many of them. Oh, my heart was so full of emotion. I cried and felt as though I had finally come home. Once again during our trip, Alana said with concern, "Mom, are you okay?"

"Alana, these are *our* ancestors. This is where our great-great-great grandparents and countless aunts and uncles and cousins are buried, right here. I can't believe we found them. I'm so happy we kept looking. I feel somehow complete and our journey over here was worth it in so many ways," I said, with tears rolling down my cheeks. "I am so very grateful that you are here with me to experience this wonderful and glorious day. You are my firstborn and when I first held you, it was magical, just like this day."

I hugged my daughter tightly and felt pure joy and profound love—for her, my husband, my other children, and all my ancestors who lived before me in Ireland. We caught up with the Flood family as we entered the Clonmacnoise Interpretive Center. We paid the visitor's fee to the clerk at the counter. I needed to come clean; my Catholic conscience had caught up with me. We told the Floods about the wondrous finding of our ancestors, and they were happy for us. We exchanged addresses, emails, and promises to stay in touch. Our meeting was so touching that I never wanted to forget it. And I didn't. For the last eight years, we have exchanged Christmas cards with that special family. I will always remember the extraordinary night and morning we spent together in the midlands of Ireland.

CHAPTER 14
Dublin

W E WERE SAD TO LEAVE Clonmacnoise Monastery and our newfound friends, but we had to drive to Dublin for the last leg of our journey. The city was eighty miles to the east. I had gained confidence driving in Ireland, but that assurance was slowly waning as thoughts of driving in its biggest city began to creep into my brain.

The once-stormy day turned into a brilliantly sunny one as we drove along the two-lane highway. About an hour out of Dublin, the road became a real highway with three lanes in each direction. Hailing from California, I found it very unusual to drive on a freeway with so few cars. On the outskirts of Dublin, traffic increased, and I began to get very nervous. My goal was to drive directly to the hotel, park our car, and become a pedestrian again.

We found the Leeson Street Inn and a parking space nearby fairly easily. We were able to check into our room early and drop off our luggage. Decorated in shades of gray, lavender, and black, our room was chic and modern. The inn was located one block from St. Stephen's Green, a large park in the heart of Dublin. We specifically chose this location because it was within walking distance of places we wanted to visit. We left the inn with a city map in hand, ready to sightsee.

We walked through the southeast corner of the park and enjoyed the beauty of the manicured lawns, statues, and lovely fountains. The green today is a far cry from the marshy common area where the townspeople once let their cattle graze.

Starting in 1664, plots of land surrounding the green were sold to well-to-do people. Eventually, Georgian-style houses were erected. Only the wealthy were allowed access to the park until 1877. An act of Parliament, initiated by Sir Alec Guinness of the brewing family, declared it a public place. He contributed money to the green's redesign and then donated the park to the people of Dublin. St. Stephen's Green was dedicated on July 27, 1880.

We exited through the Fusiliers' Arch on the northwest corner onto Grafton Street. The arch honors the Royal Dublin Fusiliers who fought and died in the Second Boer War from 1899-1900.

Their names are engraved on the monument. Erected in 1907, it was modeled from the Arch of Titus in Rome.

We headed to the Temple Bar area of Dublin, several blocks from Dame Street. This section was first identified on a map in 1674. It is thought to have been named after the provost of Trinity College, Sir William Temple, whose house and gardens were located in the area. The Temple Bar area is now known not only for its nightlife and bars but also for its cultural events. It is one of the medieval areas of Dublin where the cobblestone streets and old buildings remain.

As we walked up Grafton Street to Temple Bar, we noticed many high-end clothing shops much like Stanford Shopping Center in Palo Alto, California.

Alana and I aren't really into that sort of thing, but we had fun people watching instead. The Dublin women like to dress, and their outfits fascinated us. One young woman walking in front of us was wearing black tights and a long gold knit sweater that barely covered her bottom. It had an extremely low cowl back that dropped down to the top of her tights at her waist, showing the top of her tights and black bra. I just kept thinking, she has got to be cold in that outfit, and what was she thinking when she put that on?

Alana and I were getting hungry. We easily found a vegetarian restaurant in the big city. Looking at the menu's offerings visible behind the glass counter, much of the food was unfamiliar to me. I had to look up and read the ingredients in each of the dishes posted on the wall behind the counter. The truly vegetarian restaurants are quite creative with their vegetable mixtures. This was one of those places. Since Alana had been a vegetarian for several years, she ordered quickly. I found a dish that looked good to me, and I asked the employee, "Can I have the dish with the garbanzo beans in it please?" I pointed at it with my index finger.

"Would yu say tha' again?" said the young man with a ponytail.

"Sure, that one there, with the garbanzo beans, please."

"Oh, is tha' what yu call chickpeas in America?" he said smiling.

"Yes, that's what I call them, anyway."

"Hey, can yu please say that word to my co-worker, let me go get her."

"Sure." I watched him run to the back of the restaurant and come out with a young, attractive woman in tow.

"Miss, can yu please say that word again?" he said.

"Sure. Garbanzo beans," I said, feeling a bit silly.

The young woman smiled and laughed. "'Tis sure a funny word, tha' one."

"Yes, I guess it is," I said to them as the young man finally handed me my order from behind the counter. I sat down next to Alana, who was already eating. I told her about my experience with the restaurant employees. It was eye-opening to be the foreigner for once and the source of amusement because of my American accent and speech. She laughed.

We finished our delicious lunch and walked out into the Irish sunshine. Everyone on the streets seemed to be in a good mood. The weather was perfect on December 29, which was enough to make anyone feel jolly in Ireland.

CHAPTER 15
National Museum

W E WOKE UP EARLY KNOWING we were
going to have a busy day in Dublin. After a
delicious breakfast downstairs at our inn, we began
our day by walking east towards the National
Museum of Ireland, which houses the
archaeological wonders of the country.

Alana and I both enjoy looking at artifacts and
reading about history, so we were eager to see what
was on exhibition at the museum. Located on
Kildare Street, the museum is several blocks from
the Leeson Inn and St. Stephen's Green. On
Saturday, the 30th of December 2006, the museum
was to open at 10:00 a.m., and we wanted to be
there when it did.

As we entered the building, we scanned the
information board for interesting exhibits. Two in

particular that caught our attention were the "Ór Gold" and the "Bog Bodies of Ireland" exhibits.

We began on the ground floor with the Ór exhibit. Behind the sparkling glass cases were gold artifacts, some dating back to 2200 BC. This beautiful jewelry was discovered within the last 100 years, most being extracted from Ireland's peat bogs. There were so many gorgeous pieces. I was amazed at the proliferation of gold in ancient Ireland. I had read about explorers trying to find El Dorado, the city of gold in South America. It struck me funny because I think the conquistadors missed the mark. By what I saw, the golden city was in Ireland.

On display were gold collars called lunulae. The collars were made from flat sheets of gold, which were hammered, cut into crescent shapes, and worn on a person's upper chest and around the neck. Also displayed were torcs, ornate pieces made a thousand years later using a new technique for the time. Torcs were made by taking long bands of gold and twisting them together to create a semicircular necklace, armlet, or bracelet. Some were designed with the heads of animals at either end; when worn, the heads would face each other in the front of the neck or arm. Then, around AD 900, the jewelry style began to change again. Solid gold pieces were made by smelting the ore and casting the gold by pouring it into molds to form different shapes. Cloak fasteners were among the items made this way. Circular in shape, they had a separate pin that pierced the cloth, fastening it together. Delicate ear spools were fashioned using the same process. These circular gold pieces were placed inside stretched earlobes. You see many young people wearing them today, but now they are usually made of plastic or ceramic clay.

As Alana and I approached the Bog Bodies of Ireland exhibit, we were impressed by the museum's creativity. The curators of the museum, realizing that not all visitors would be comfortable seeing preserved human remains, built spiral ramps around each displayed body. Wooden slatted screens obstructed the view of museum visitors unless they chose to walk directly into the enclosure. Farmers plowing their fields or cutting the peat for their fires unearthed these incredible finds. These ancient bodies absolutely fascinated me.

One individual, Clonycavan Man, was particularly lifelike. The radiocarbon dating suggested that he lived sometime between 392-201 BC. His coiffed hair had some kind of resin in it to hold it in place. The bog perfectly preserved the stubble of a new beard on his chin as well as the nails on his fingers. Even his skin, although stained by the tannins of the peat bog, was smooth. When the scientists examined the corpse, they discovered that Clonycavan Man met a violent death. He sustained three head injuries and one to the chest. I stood mesmerized by this being who lived thousands of years ago. I wondered, what was his real name?

When we had our fill of this wonderful museum, we walked the few blocks to Trinity College to view the Book of Kells. This is one of the most celebrated illuminated manuscripts ever created. We were so excited to see it. At the entrance was a sign that read: Book of Kells exhibit is closed Christmas week from December 23-January 2.

"You're kidding me," I exclaimed.

Alana, who was practically in tears, said, "No, no. I have always wanted to see this book. We came so far and we are going to miss it."

She was a book art minor at Mills College in Oakland at the time and had created a few books herself. It was a bitter disappointment to her. "Well, we are just going to have to come back to Ireland again, Alana."

"Yes, we'll have to come back, Mom," Alana sighed.

An Irish woman overheard us talking and said cheerfully, "Oh lass, I know yur disappointed, but thur's another place nearby with wonderful fancy buks called the Chester Beatty Library. It's only few blocks away, near Dublin Castle."

"Really? Thank you so much," Alana said. So, off we trotted down Ship Street to the library.

When we entered, we were not disappointed. Hundreds of beautifully illustrated books from all over the world were on display, including gorgeous manuscripts from Persia, China, and Japan. Delicate, miniature paintings were among the lovely and varied artwork. Alana and I felt this experience truly made up for missing out on the Book of Kells.

Our last stop that day was St. Patrick's Cathedral, just a few blocks away from the library. Erected in AD 1220, it was quite beautiful. It was built in the traditional shape of the cross. The stained glass windows above the altar were exquisite. As the sun penetrated the glass, the colors of the rainbow were brought to life inside the church. I lit a candle for my sister Peggy, who passed away in 2000. This gesture brought me peace. We walked up and down the aisles, gazing at the statues of the saints. Many famous people were buried there including Jonathan Swift, author of *Gulliver's Travels.*

At this point, we were getting quite tuckered out. We still had to drive to our new place of lodging, a B&B called the Annagh House. It was several miles away in the Clontarf section of the city across from Dublin Bay. As we drove up, we were pleased find a Victorian-style building painted a cheerful sunny yellow. When we saw the interior elegantly decorated in antiques, we were in heaven. John, the innkeeper, greeted us. "Hello, Ladies, yu must be Mary and Alana," he said cheerfully. "Wud yu care for a cuppa tea?" He had the tea ready because I had given him our planned time of arrival the day before.

"Oh, yes. That would be lovely," I said gratefully. We've had a very long day exploring Dublin. What an amazing city."

"Ah, tha' 'tis. Where did yu go?'

"Well, we went to the National Museum of History and saw the Bog Bodies. They were so fascinating. And we saw the Ór Gold exhibit there too, so much gold. I had no idea there was so much in Ireland," I said with surprise.

"Ah, yes. People don't realize what amazin' treasures we have here."

"We also went to the Chester Beatty Library and saw so many gorgeous books," Alana piped in.

"Anythin' else?" said John.

"Yes, St. Patrick's Cathedral. That was so lovely."

"It sounds like yu Ladies covered a lot of ground today," John said pleasingly. "Enjoy yur tea

Ladies and take yur time."

"What a nice man, isn't he Alana?"

"Yes, he is Mom. I really enjoy staying at B&Bs. They are so cozy. And the innkeepers are all so nice."

We sat back and drank our Irish tea savoring the beautiful inn and all its contents. It was truly a glorious day in Dublin.

CHAPTER 16
An Irish New Year's Eve

THE ANNAGH HOUSE WAS A wonderful place to stay. We woke up and enjoyed a scrumptious Irish breakfast. Because we now knew what was included in an Irish breakfast, we made sure to tell them the night before to skip the black and white puddings.

John and Delia Devlin, who owned and ran the inn, were very hospitable people. They suggested we take the bus into the main part of the city instead of driving. Needless to say, I liked the idea. The bus stop was conveniently located a few blocks away, and the bus ride itself was straightforward.

It was December 31, New Year's Eve. We couldn't believe our visit had gone by so quickly. Our mission today was to shop for gifts for our family and friends. Alana and I hadn't shopped much on our trip. Today was our last day in Ireland, so it needed to be done. We were looking for Christmas gifts that were definitely of Irish origin. The other requirement was that they be lightweight, since I had only brought a backpack for my two-week stay.

We headed to Grafton Street, the main shopping area in Dublin. The street runs from St. Stephen's Green in the south to College Green to the north. It has many wonderful shops with all kinds of lovely merchandise. Strolling down the street, Alana and I saw a bronze statue in the distance. As we got closer, we could see it was of a young woman dressed in seventeenth century clothing—Molly Malone. We were so excited. One of my favorite songs, I had taught "Molly Malone" to my preschool students over the years. I had always loved the song, because it was written about an Irish woman. Here is the first verse, in case you have never heard it before:

In Dublin's fair city, where the girls are so pretty,
I first set my eyes on sweet Molly Malone.
As she wheeled her wheelbarrow,
through the streets broad and narrow,
Crying, "Cockles and mussels, alive, alive, oh."
"Alive, alive, oh. Alive, alive, oh."
Crying, "Cockles and muscles, Alive, alive, oh."

The bronzed Molly was dressed quite scantily in a low-cut blouse. She is known in Dublin as "The Tart with a Cart"; "The Dish with a Fish"; "The Trollop with a Scallop"; "The Dolly with a Trolley"; and "The Flirt with a Skirt." Dubliners have justified the skimpiness of her attire. In the seventeenth century, women publicly breastfed their children, and the style of women's clothing at the time showed a lot of breast.

We went into many shops looking for the perfect gifts. I found a great store, which carried an abundance of wool scarves in many different hues and plaids. I had fun choosing the colors that suited each of my loved ones. They were truly the right presents for my sons, brothers, and sisters.

I love to see Irishmen in their wool Paddy caps, so I bought a handsome moss green tweed hat for my beloved husband, Duane. For my childhood friend, Lisa, I bought a ceramic thimble with a Claddagh symbol on it. The design is comprised of two hands holding a heart with a crown on top. The hands symbolize friendship; the heart, love; and the crown, loyalty. Because Lisa and I had learned how to sew together, the thimble was a perfect present for one of my oldest friends.

While we were shopping, Alana received a call from her friend Steph, who had been touring Ireland as well. She, too, was leaving the next day.

Alana got off the phone and said, "Mom, Steph wants to know if she can stay at the inn with us. She has called many inns and they are all full because it's New Year's Eve."

"Well, it's fine with me, but I need to call the inn and ask John if it would be all right."

I called the inn right away and said, "John, a friend of Alana's has no place to stay. Can she sleep in our room? She has nowhere else to go."

"Sure, Mary, tha' 'tis fine. I am going to charge her thirty Euros fur the night. I hope tha' 'tis okay with hur."

"I am sure that will be fine, John. I will have Alana call her and I will get back to you."

I felt that was fair, and we called Steph back to let her know. She was very happy. We were to meet Steph on the O'Connell Bridge over the Liffey River at 4:00 p.m., then she would come back to the inn with us. Alana and I were exhausted from shopping as we waited on the bridge with our purchases in hand. It was very cold that day, and the wind was blowing fiercely. It began to sprinkle and then rain.

"Alana, Steph better get here really quick because this weather is about to get worse," I said with exasperation.

"I know Mom. I'll call her again." The next thing we saw was poor Steph, dragging her humongous suitcase over the old bridge. We ran to help her and headed straight to the bus stop. Once inside the comfy bus, we chatted happily all the way to the inn.

"Mary, thank you sooo much for letting me stay with you and Alana."

"Steph, I am happy to help out. We can't have you staying out on the streets on a cold and rainy New Year's Eve. We have plenty of space in our room for you."

Upon our return, we got Steph settled in our room, and we all went downstairs to have her meet the innkeepers. Once again, John and Delia had our tea ready for us.

"Nice to meet yu, Steph. We heard yu've been travlin' around Ireland by yurself."

"Yes, I have, and it has been wonderful. The people are so kind here."

"Ah, tha' they are, tha' they are. Where was yur favorite place?" asked Delia.

"The Aran Islands," Steph said.

John shook his head and said, "Ah, yes, the Aran Islands are remarkable."

"Where are yu plannin' tu eat dinner tonight Ladies?" asked John.

"I have no idea. Any suggestions?" I said.

"Wull, thur's a nice Indian places a few doors down. I can call fur a table?"

"That would be perfect. How about dinner at 7:00 p.m.?"

"I wull make the call right now. 'Tis a busy night New Year's Eve and all." He rushed off to make the call while we sipped our lovely hot tea.

Thankfully, the rain had stopped and we walked the thirty steps down the road to the restaurant. We had a delicious meal of yellow curry, korma, masala, and rice. I splurged on an Australian bottle of Shiraz to commemorate the ending of our journey and to celebrate New Year's Eve.

After dinner, we headed back to Annagh House and played my travel Scrabble game until twelve o'clock. Earlier in the evening, I had gotten directions to the airport, paid our room bill, and said our goodbyes and thank yous to John and Delia.

At the stroke of midnight, we hugged and laughed and then went to bed. Alana and I had to wake up at 5:00 a.m. to make a 7:30 a.m. flight to New York. Steph's plane was taking off a few hours later, so she got to sleep in.

That morning, it was spooky driving to the airport in the dark. I had pretty much avoided driving at night in Ireland. I made a few wrong turns but finally got us to the airport safe and sound. Dropping off our car at the rental agency, I was relieved to return the car in one piece.

As Alana and I sat and waited for our flight back to the States, we began to reminisce about our adventures in Ireland. Rambling through the Emerald Isle with my daughter, Alana, continues to be one of the most memorable events of my life.

CHAPTER 17
A Gift, in More Ways Than One

WHEN I BOARDED THE LUFTHANSA aircraft eight years ago, headed for Frankfurt, Germany, I was sobbing. I looked back at Duane and my three young sons, and felt physical pain. I was torn about going away at Christmas time. I felt guilty, but Duane insisted that I go. I had flown by myself several times, but never out of the United States. Flying to a foreign land made me feel extremely vulnerable.

When I arrived in Germany, I felt scared and alone, like a fox that had fallen down a deep hole and couldn't climb out. Most of the people in the airport were speaking German or another foreign language. Now, I know how people from other countries feel when they come to America and don't speak English. It was an "aha" moment for me. When I finally connected with Alana, I felt more at ease seeing a familiar face.

The next challenge I encountered on the trip was driving in Ireland. Duane did most of the driving back home when we went long distances, so I wasn't used to that responsibility. Ireland was a double whammy because I had to drive on the opposite side of the road, which took a lot of guts. By the third day of driving in Ireland, I felt more confident.

Marriage can be a wonderful experience, but sometimes a woman becomes too dependent upon her husband, which I'll admit, happened to me. I had been an independent young woman and somewhere along the line, I lost confidence with driving and making important decisions. When Duane told me about the trip, I felt petrified to go without him. It took a lot of convincing on his part to get me to agree to go. Isn't it strange how we can want something so badly, but when it is handed to us, we become afraid?

I realized that the selfless gift Duane gave to me taught me several valuable lessons. By sending me to Europe on a plane by myself, I had to face my fear of being without him, which was a real possibility in the near future. His gift caused me to stand on my own two feet and realize that I was capable of living without him.

My transformation was apparent. I grew more confident. I knew I would be able to take care of myself and my children and that I wouldn't fall apart. I began to go places by myself. I became aware of the importance to have my own interests that were different from Duane's. My husband's gift helped me recapture a part of myself that had begun to fade away. This was an important lesson he had taught me, but I didn't realize he was teaching it to me.

I do know that after his surgery, I noticed a change in me, that I was stronger, emotionally. I also became aware that I didn't get upset anymore when he made plans with his friends to golf or go on a hike without me. I didn't need to spend every waking hour with him to feel loved. My insecurities had dissipated, and I felt content with myself. What a wonderful gift Duane gave me, in more ways than one.

EPILOGUE

I T HAS BEEN EIGHT YEARS since I journeyed to Ireland with my daughter. Alana and I came back home to the U.S. on January 1, 2007. Three weeks later, Duane, had his spleen removed. The surgery was supposed to take only three hours but ended up taking five and one-half hours, and I was getting very nervous.

Finally, Duane's surgeon, Dr. Rockson Liu, came out looking haggard and said, "Mrs. Heaton, it was the most difficult laparoscopic splenectomy I have ever done. He needed two blood transfusions, but he is stable now."

That was music to my ears. I was so relieved. He made it through the operation.

Three more years passed and Duane continued to be in remission. In June of 2010, we went on a three-week vacation to Italy with our two youngest children, Colton and Sam, and had a wonderful time. We returned in July. One month later, Duane received news from his doctor that the lymphoma had returned.

Duane had more successful chemotherapy from February to July of 2011 as requested by his new oncologist, Dr. Huang. As of September 2014, he was still in remission. We are very grateful to all the doctors and nurses who have helped Duane over these last nine years.

IN 2010, I DECIDED TO get my DNA tested. I had seen an Oprah TV episode where Dr. Louis Gates, a Harvard professor, was talking about genealogy and DNA testing. I looked up the DNA company, 23andMe, online and sent for a DNA test kit. Three weeks after spitting into a test tube, I received my DNA information. The results were quite outstanding. Not only did I find out about my mother's ancestry, I also received medical information about which diseases I am at risk of developing.

My one disappointment was that I could only learn of my maternal ancestry, since I had taken a mitochondrial DNA test. Unlike chromosomal DNA, which is inherited from both parents, everyone gets their mitochondrial DNA from only one parent—their mother. In order to find out my entire genetic picture, I needed to have one of my brother's DNA tested too. So, for my brother Mark's fiftieth birthday, I bought him a kit.

Well, it was so much fun talking with my brother when we received his DNA results because we found out that we are related to one of the High Kings of Ireland. His name was King Niall or O'Neill, as it is now spelled. My great-grandmother was Margaret (Peggy) O'Neill. She was born in Galway, Ireland, to Jeremiah O'Neill and Kathleen (née Carroll) O'Neill. It is this line which carries back to my ancestor King Niall, one of the High Kings of Tara, who reigned from AD 379 - 405. Ui'Niall means descendants of Niall. They ruled Ireland until the eleventh century.

King Niall raided Britain, Wales, and France, where he established small kingdoms. He had twelve sons, each of whom became powerful kings in their own right. He came to be known as "Niall Noigiallach" which means "Niall of the Nine Hostages." This was based on the fact he took hostages from other Irish royal families, as well as from Britain and the European mainland, to subdue his enemies. Niall was also said to have captured St. Patrick, then a slave, and brought him back to Ireland.

Niall's DNA is most prolific in Northwest Ireland where one in five males carry his

Y chromosome. In Scotland, one in ten men carry it, and in the U.S., 2% of New Yorkers carry his DNA. Researchers at Trinity College's Smurfit Institute in Dublin estimated there are approximately three million men alive today carrying King Niall's Y chromosome. He is second only to Genghis Khan as the most fertile man that ever lived with sixteen million male descendants.

At the beginning of summer in 2014, my Aunt Jane and Cousin Terry and her daughter, Tara, traveled to Ireland. Since Terry had edited my book, she visited many of the places in Ireland I described in my memoir. While she was at Clonmacnoise, she met up with a docent who showed her where the Claffey tombstones were located. The docent also told her that one of the stone churches, Dowling Church, was originally named, Mac Claffey's Church, and was built in the tenth century. I had no idea that the prefix, Mac, was originally placed before the surname, Claffey. It has opened up my research of the Claffey descendants. Mac Claffey means son of a chief or prince. So, once again, there is royal Irish blood in my ancestry. I am eager to find out more about the Mac Claffey line.

Through my brother Mark's DNA results, I also learned that my father's parents were originally Celts from Ireland too. (This makes sense since

European countries are close together, and these seafaring people could migrate easily.) My paternal grandparents did not share their language or culture with my dad though they were born in Denmark. I've always felt sad not to know my dad's parents, and I have read about Denmark and its culture to make up for that loss. Perhaps a trip to Denmark will help me to connect to my Scandinavian roots.

Now, I have come full circle. I feel more content since I've come back from Ireland knowing more about my family tree both historically and genetically. What a wonderful journey.

Mary Heaton
July 30, 2014

ACKNOWLEDGEMENT

The writing of this memoir would not have been possible without these wonderful people who helped me along the way.

First and foremost, I need to thank my husband, Duane, because without his selfless love, this memoir would not exist. Next, I want to thank Alana, a wonderful daughter and traveling companion who loves Ireland just as much as I do. I am grateful to my sons, Amando, Colton, and Sam, and my daughter, Jill, for understanding why I had to go to Ireland during their Christmas break and being okay with it.

Many thanks go to my writing teacher, Susan Wilson, who provided me with a safe and encouraging environment to write my stories. I wish to thank my classmates who listened each week to my chapters about Ireland with patience and enthusiasm.

I am indebted to my friend of many years, Sandi Pack, who was the first to read my memoir from start to finish and encouraged me to publish it. My friend and former colleague from Valley Montessori School, Kellie Essary, took the time to both copy-edit the first draft and teach me the subtleties of punctuation, and I am very grateful to her. A very special thank you goes to my newly-acquainted cousin, Terry Tunnington, for meticulously reading, making corrections, and emailing me with her helpful thoughts about each chapter. Terry graciously allowed me to put twenty of her lovely photos of Ireland in my memoir. The cover photo is hers too and it is absolutely beautiful. Also, thanks go to her husband Rick, who checked for those pesky typos and continuity.

I would like to thank my dear friend, Cris Cassell, for reading my memoir and helping me recognize the themes of family, food and history.

I want to express my enduring gratitude to all my lovely friends. (You know who you are.) You have stood by me in this journey we call life. You've been there in times of grief, when I lost my parents and siblings, Peggy, Patrick, and Katy. You've also shared those memorable celebrations in times of joy. I thank you with all my heart.

To my siblings, Colleen, Chris, and Mark, thank you for watching over me while I grew up. I have learned many invaluable lessons from you. I love you all.

And lastly, I offer my heartfelt gratitude to the matriarch of the Claffy Clan, my Aunt Jane. You are a gift from God to my entire family and me. Words alone can't express how much I love you. You have been my rock and savior on many occasions. I admire your sense of humor, intelligence, and compassion. I have tried my best to emulate you in my life.

Mary Heaton

ABOUT THE AUTHOR

Mary Heaton grew up in Livermore, California, with her six siblings, and as her mother used to say, "There is never a dull moment." These memorable childhood experiences presented Mary with a great deal of writing material from which to choose.

Mary is a retired Montessori teacher, who has an innate love of learning, which she has shared with her children and hundreds of students over the years. It was only five years ago she started to capture her stories on paper.

Mary's passions are her five amazing children, writing in the wee hours of the morning, gardening in the shade of her sycamore trees, singing to hospice patients, practicing yoga with enlightened friends, swimming for miles, and hosting Chinese international students in her home.

Mary is a published author of short stories and poetry. She received a certificate of recognition during a reading at Las Positas College for her story published in their 2014 Anthology.

She lives in her dream house, a 120-year-old Victorian in Livermore, with her beloved husband, Duane, their youngest son, Sam, and dog, Sophie. *Rambling Through the Emerald Isle* is her first book.

CPSIA information can be obtained at www.ICGtesting.com
Printed in the USA
BVOW07s0008261214

380831BV00001B/1/P